The Hague Academy's Lectures on Emmanuel Gaillard's Legacy

Les Conférences de l'Académie sur l'héritage scientifique d'Emmanuel Gaillard

ISBN 978-90-04-68739-4

Imprimé par/Printed by Triangle Bleu, Maubeuge, France

The Hague Academy's Lectures
on Emmanuel Gaillard's Legacy

Les Conférences de l'Académie
sur l'héritage scientifique d'Emmanuel Gaillard

Emmanuel Gaillard

GENERAL TABLE OF CONTENTS

TABLE GÉNÉRALE DES MATIÈRES

TABLE OF CONTENTS
TABLE DES MATIÈRES

FOREWORD

The Hague Academy of International Law is the place par excellence where international law is taught, disseminated, discussed and critiqued. It is also where the key ideas on which academic debate, and sometimes international practice, are often formulated. These ideas can be followed, developed and nuanced – in short, they can "set the standard" – but they can also, of course, be challenged with varying degrees of intensity.

The special course given to the Academy by Professor Emmanuel Gaillard in the mid-2000s is a notable illustration of this. Published not only in the *Recueil des cours* but also in the Academy's very first Pocket Book, this lecture entitled "Philosophical Aspects of International Arbitration Law" has become a "classic" for anyone wishing to understand something about international arbitration. It is also at the centre of a fairly lively academic debate which, in essence, amounts to questioning the real merits of international arbitration conceived as grounded on an autonomous legal order.

The Academy was therefore delighted to invite Professor Gaillard to give the General Course on Private International Law in the summer of 2022. In fact, this course had long been scheduled to be given the previous year, in 2021, but the Covid-19 health crisis postponed all schedules by a year. Mrs Banifatemi, in her lecture published in this book, refers to the direction that Professor Gaillard chose to take with his General Course, which he had entitled "The New Theory of Conflicts of Systems: National Legal Orders and Arbitral Legal Order".

Fate has deprived us of this reflection that he had been pondering over for a long time and which he was delighted to develop for our Attendees in the magnificent Auditorium of the Academy, which is more "for" the Academy for which he had the friendliest thoughts. We were as delighted as he was.

During the summer of 2022, the Academy paid him a special tribute by organising a series of five lectures devoted to his ideas and work, given by Professors Horatia Muir Watts, Diego P. Fernández Arroyo, Luca G. Radicati di Brozolo, Mrs Yas Banifatemi and Judge Dominique Hascher.

The texts of these lectures are reproduced in this book, which the Academy dedicates to the loving memory of Professor Emmanuel Gaillard.

PRÉFACE

L'Académie est le lieu par excellence où le droit international s'enseigne, se diffuse, se discute, et se critique. Y sont aussi souvent formulées les idées fortes à partir desquelles le débat académique, et parfois aussi la pratique internationale, s'ordonne durablement. Elles peuvent être suivies, développées, nuancées, en somme « faire école », mais aussi, bien sûr, être la source d'un rejet plus ou moins vif.

Le cours spécial donné au milieu des années 2000 à l'Académie par le Professeur Emmanuel Gaillard en est une notable illustration. Publié non seulement dans le *Recueil des cours* mais aussi dans le tout premier Livre de Poche de l'Académie, ce cours intitulé « Aspects philosophiques du droit de l'arbitrage international » est devenu un « classique » pour qui entend comprendre quelque chose à l'arbitrage international. Il est aussi au centre d'un débat académique assez vif qui, au fond, revient à s'interroger sur les mérites réels de l'arbitrage international entendu comme reposant sur un ordre juridique autonome.

C'est dire que l'Académie se réjouissait de l'invitation du Professeur Gaillard à donner le cours général de droit international privé à l'été 2022. A vrai dire, ce cours avait été programmé de longue date pour être donné l'année précédente, en 2021, mais la crise sanitaire du Covid-19 avait repoussé toutes les programmations d'une année. Mme Banifatemi, dans sa conférence publiée dans cet ouvrage, fait référence au tour que le Professeur Gaillard avait choisi de donner à son cours général qu'il avait intitulé « La nouvelle théorie des conflits des ordres : ordres juridiques étatiques et ordre juridique arbitral ».

Le destin nous a privés de cette réflexion qu'il mûrissait depuis longtemps et dont il se réjouissait de la développer pour nos auditeurs dans le magnifique Auditorium de l'Académie, qui plus est « pour » l'Académie pour laquelle il nourrissait les pensées les plus amicales. Nous nous en réjouissions tout autant que lui.

Durant l'été 2022, l'Académie lui a rendu un hommage spécial en organisant un cycle de cinq conférences consacrées à sa pensée et à son œuvre, données par les Professeurs Horatia Muir Watt, Diego P. Fernández Arroyo, Luca G. Radicati di Brozolo, Mme Yas Banifatemi, et M. le juge Dominique Hascher.

Les textes de ces conférences sont reproduits dans cet ouvrage que l'Académie dédie à la mémoire que nous conservons intacte du Professeur Emmanuel Gaillard.

TAKING E. GAILLARD'S POST-WESTPHALIAN PARADIGM SERIOUSLY

by

Horatia Muir Watt *

Continuing a conversation . . . Emmanuel Gaillard was always open to courteous discussion (even when he remained unconvinced!). What follows is an attempt to revitalise a conversation that began a very long time ago, on whether there exists such a thing as a "philosophy" of international arbitration (and, if it exists, what it might look like [1]). The specific focus here is the concept of an autonomous arbitral legal order, freed from the tutorship of state, as it appears in his widely read Hague lectures [2]. It is certainly a tribute to Gaillard's rhetorical talent that such a concept is now something of a fetiche in recent (particularly continental) doctrines of international arbitration. Such accounts appeal unquestioningly to this form of free-standing legality in framing the relationship between formal (state) and informal (arbitral or other) legal orders [3]. The arbitrator is increasingly represented as the "natural forum" for transnational legal disputes and takes precedence in various instances over state courts, with or without the help of the latter themselves [4].

---

* Professor, Science Po Law School, Paris.

1. For evidence of this conversation see D. Bureau and H. Muir Watt, *Droit international privé*, 5th ed 2021 (para. 891, Vol. II, unchanged since 2nd ed.).

2. "Aspects philosophiques du droit de l'arbitrage international", *Recueil des cours*, tome 329 (2007).

3. Often in the name of the nebulous principle of "party autonomy", that harks back discursively (and often confusedly) to much earlier doctrines borrowed from classical liberal thought and determinative of the regulatory emancipation of international contracts, including the agreement to arbitrate. The critique of party autonomy in private international law is too well known to warrant detailed references here. However, for a fresh philosophical look at the misuse of the concept of autonomy (often used to mean the contrary of what it signified in the context of liberal theory), see C. Pelluchon, *Les Lumières à l'Age du Vivant*, Seuil, 2021. And for a broad critique of neoliberal legality, little cited in the private international law literature, see H. Brabazon (ed.), *Neoliberal Legality: Understanding the Role of Law in the Neoliberal Project*, New York, Routledge, 2016.

4. This special status of arbitration transpires through devices such as (negative and positive), *Kompetenz-Kompetenz*, but also *res judicata* and issue estoppel, *autorité de la chose arbitrée*, appeals for universalising *lis pendens*, theories of inherent jurisdictional powers, vocation to emit anti-suit injunctions to concurrent proceedings in state courts etc.

Gaillard's claim: a new paradigm of legality. Gaillard himself chose to locate his claim on the jurisprudential terrain of jurisdiction [5]. As his claim goes, the very foundation of the arbitrator's authority lies in a legal arrangement that exists beyond or outside the state [6]. Indeed, he maintains, the "Westphalian" paradigm of legality cannot account for a series of signals or symptoms (emerging from the practice of state courts or arbitral tribunals [7]) that point to the emergence of what might be seen as a new constitutional foundation for private international ordering. Such a claim is nothing short of a redefinition of our legal world, or *nomos*, as detached from state [8]. Undoubtedly, this redefinition is in itself an important and convincing move. Our "era of the post" [9] calls into question modernity's epistemological and ontological premises in meaningful and salutary ways, including those underlying our conceptions of law as indissolubly tied to the (modern, Western) state form.

What further implications? But here is precisely where the discussion kicks in. The very simple contention in what follows is that *if* the arbitral order is an autonomous, transnational form of legality (and not merely a further instance of contract governance), and indeed the

5. The reference here is to S. Mc Veigh (ed.), *Jurisprudence of Jurisdiction*, New York, Routledge, 2007.

6. Albeit, as we shall see, with the consensus of the community of leviathans. In a key passage, E. Gaillard writes (para. 62):

> "Dans le domaine des relations commerciales internationales, c'est la convergence des ordres juridiques étatiques qui, par l'acceptation qu'elle manifeste du phénomène arbitral, en légitime l'existence. En acceptant de confier, pour les parties qui l'ont voulu, le pouvoir de juger les différends du commerce international aux arbitres et de reconnaître le produit du processus arbitral qu'est la sentence, sans le contrôler au fond, la communauté des Etats a conféré à l'arbitrage international une réelle autonomie. Le statut de 'juge international' que certaines juridictions parmi les plus progressistes en la matière lui reconnaissent constitue la meilleure illustration du fait que l'*arbitre peut être aujourd'hui considéré comme l'organe d'un ordre juridique propre.* Dans l'exercice de cette fonction, l'arbitre international dégage des normes qui, pour être la résultante de l'activité normative des Etats, n'appartiennent en propre, en tant que normes transnationales, à aucun d'eux."

7. I do not have time to enumerate the various strands of comparative (state) case-law that addres this issue. But my intention is not to assess the conformity of Gaillard's position with contemporary or ulterior practice, which evolves continually and with which the audience is no doubt familiar. I am taking Gaillard's claim on the terrain on which he located it himself, that is, as a normative or a philosophical one.

8. On law as *nomos*, meaning the normative universe we inhabit, see R. Cover ("Nomos", 1983-4).

9. M. Xifaras, "The Global Turn in Legal Theory", *Canadian Journal of Law & Jurisprudence*, XXIX (2016), 215–243.

political-legal foundation of the arbitrator's jurisdiction, then it cannot escape the jurisprudential, normative, epistemological, and ontological issues that arise and are constantly debated in respect of legal pluralism. These enjoin (at the very least) to revisit the grounding and legitimacy of jurisdiction as embedded in other present and past informal (private or non-state) normative orders (imperial, transnational, global but also indigenous, digital or subterranean… [10]) and, above all, call for a detour beyond the monist legal paradigm and outside the legal discipline itself. In the context of our sadly unfinished conversation, it seems to me that Emmanuel Gaillard did not draw the consequences of his own critique of modern law's jurisprudential foundations [11].

Reminder: the conundrum of the status of awards. In his "Aspects Philosophiques", Gaillard presents a three-part interpretative grid designed to explain, in theoretical terms, the marked variations in the legal status of international arbitral awards before different state courts. More specifically, as is well known to you all, the conundrum that he attempted to solve related to the weight to be given in one country to the annulment of an award in another (and further still, whether or not it is important where such annulment took place). The tryptic he proposes is highly instructive in that it helps understand that the stakes underpinning such a choice are not "merely technical" [12] but have deep underlying implications that may also be viewed, as the title of his course announces, from a jurisprudential or legal-philosophical angle – or indeed (one might add) as a matter of epistemology, ontology, ethics or political economy. What he calls "mental representations" count in terms of technical-legal consequences; conversely, the latter need to be contextualised within a wider or deeper scheme of thought.

Gaillard's three-part interpretative grid. Gaillard's grid distinguishes three possible jurisprudential positions, each with its own concrete legal implications in respect of the validity of (potentially fragile) awards.

10. On the grounding of jurisdiction in early modern empire (and "interpolity" law more generally), see L. Benton, *Law and Colonial Cultures, Legal regimes in World History 1400-1900*, spec. p. 210 ss. *Constructing Sovereignty*; for an attempt to formulate a jurisprudence of global law see N. Walker, *Intimations of global law*, CUP 2015.

11. Anecdotally: by contrast to some of the usual "Westphalian" objections to his theory, based on a reluctance to abandon a state-centred model of law, my own position surprised him insofar as I found that he was not pluralist enough…

12. The reference here is to Duncan Kennedy's famous analysis of the stakes underlying the "merely technical" rules of private law in adjudication before state courts ("Form and Substance in Private Law Adjudication", 89 *Harv. L. Rev.* 1685, 1976).

The "Westphalian" paradigm covers two hypotheses [13] in which the arbitral process is viewed through the eyes of the state. It makes a difference of course as to which state in particular we are referring to. Thus, one (the more enlightened?) view is that only an annulment in the state where the legal seat of the arbitration is located is of any significance. One might say that this view resembles, in conflict of laws theory, the principle of the "competent legal order" [14], in which all states other than the one that has (under an assumed consensus, and with a generous dose of fictionality) a preeminent title to determine the validity of a legal relationship will align their positions on the latter. However, another widespread practice that appeals to legal pragmatism is to consider that the validity of the award depends directly upon any and all the local (or territorial) sovereigns called upon to enforce it [15].

The key move beyond Westphalia. The third vision can be characterised as post-Westphalian, because no longer does the state (or more correctly, no other state, not even the state of the seat) have the last word in determining the validity of the award. Indeed, what is generally meant by the "Westphalian legal order" implies a mutually exclusive relationship between law and state (there is no legality beyond the state form). This relationship is described in legal-theoretical terms as monism, because it allows for only one perspective or standpoint (that of the state) from which law can be constituted. In Gaillard's conception, however, there is no longer any rule of reference or priority in terms of the title of any state whatsoever. The legal status of an arbitration award is governed, autonomously, by a non-state legal order. Although Gaillard claimed to be strictly descriptive, he made no real secret of his preference both in policy terms and as a matter of legal theory, for the latter [16].

---

13. Only the second below is specifically labelled as such (para. 30: "le modèle westphalien: l'indifférence érigée en vertu"), but as both are state-centered, they contrast with the third, which is dissociated from any jurisdictional act "au nom d'un Etat quelconque" (para. 40).

14. P. Picone, *La méthode de la référence à l'ordre juridique compétent en droit international privé*, *Recueil des cours*, tome 197 (1986).

15. In the jurisprudence of the conflict of laws, this position recalls the argument that was at one point invoked to justify the "contrat sans loi" (versus theories that required there to be a governing state law, even independently of any objective linkage). Why bother to instate a governing law if in all events the performance of a contract will be prohibited if it runs against the public policy requirements of the recognizing state?

16. That is, "celle qui accepte de considérer que la juridicité de l'arbitrage puisse être puisée non dans un ordre juridique étatique, qu'il s'agisse de celui du siège ou de celui du ou des lieux d'exécution, mais dans un ordre juridique tiers, susceptible d'être qualifié d'ordre juridique arbitral" (para. 40).

How should we assess this claim? It seems to me that by focusing his attention on a symptom and its cure (the fate or the triumph of the litigious or wonky award) rather than on the change in the wider theoretical framework, as if the latter served the interests of the former, several significant dimensions of the legal pluralist vision are omitted. Yet they also have significant implications in respect of arbitral practice, and states' reception of arbitral decisions. Once again, as Gaillard himself emphasises, ideas (mental representations) count in concrete juridical terms. To be (very) short, taking Gaillard's hypothesis seriously means making three main points. The first questions as a matter of "jurisdictional jurisprudence" [17] the very foundations of an autonomous arbitral legal order (Chap. I). The second is methodological. It argues as a matter of epistemological consistency that legal pluralism cannot be selective (Chap. II). This leads to the third point, the telos of the so-called autonomous arbitral order. It asks why the radical political economic critique in the field of investment arbitration has not carried over into the commercial field and suggests that the supposed autonomy of an arbitral legal order both rests on and reinforces the classical distinction – yet emblematic today of neoliberal legal consciousness [18] – between law and politics (Chap. III).

---

17. The reference is to the book bearing this title and edited by S. McVeigh, *op. cit.*
18. On the forms of neo-liberal legality more generally, see H. Brabazon, *op. cit.*

CHAPTER I

FOUNDATIONS: NATURALISING THE "ARBITRAL ORDER"

The quest for legitimacy. Gaillard's chosen philosophical or legal-theoretical terrain is, as we have seen, that of jurisdictional jurisprudence. The legitimacy of the arbitrator's jurisdictional function (he suggests) is unassailable, given the broad trend towards the recognition of the legitimacy of recourse to international arbitration as a (the) mode of resolution of international commercial disputes [19]. By virtue of such a trend, he suggests, arbitrators have become the natural or "proper" fora for transnational economic disputes, jurisdictional organs or agents of the international community [20]. This organic conception can be traced back to the contribution of Berthold Goldman – Gaillard's own mentor – to the famous *lex mercatoria* debate that accompanied the early soaring of postwar arbitration as a core transnational institution. Whatever the terms of this controversy, the imaginary of the arbitrator as the natural organ that speaks the law in the name and for the benefit of the "international community" does appear to be a particularly potent (and indeed literal) example of a process of "naturalisation", whereby the state of affairs purportedly "described" is slowly taken for granted, as if it was a (natural) given (and not a construct). The outcome is a wide adhesion to the implicit assumption that international arbitration participates in a "natural order" commited to a form of crossborder justice [21].

Bracketing some potential blindspots. Of course, there are many questions that come immediately to mind in respect of the foundations of the arbitral order as formulated above. One might wonder for instance how the autonomy of a non-state legal order sits with the hypothesis (requirement or fact?) that the latter draws or reinforces its

19. "Aspects philosophiques", para. 40.

20. On the arbitrator as "l'organe d'un ordre juridique propre", *ibid.*, para. 62, 127.

21. The notion of cross-border justice recalls the somewhat elusive concept of "conflicts justice" in private international law. This is (very) possibly an echo of the work of A. Von Mehren and D. Trautmann, whom Emmanuel greatly admired, at the time these scholars from the United States were very active at The Hague Conference for private international law, bringing with them the new methodologies that were progressively to become so influential in comparative, regional and supranational legislation.

authority from a consensus between sovereign leviathans. Within the grid, he opposes such an agreement to the will of any one sovereign in isolation. However, thereupon a further difficulty arises as to the identity or composition of the collective entity labelled the "international community". The answer stands on high ethical ground. It is composed of the "most progressive" of states, in whose name and interests the arbitrator purportedly acts [22]. "Progressive" here is associated with a willingness to leave the tired Westphalian sovereign by the wayside and make way for arbitral autonomy. According to Gaillard, then, the arbitrator's jurisdictional function is exercised in the service of the very states whose combined benevolence towards arbitration and its emancipation provides the political foundation of the autonomous order [23]. Such an argument seems somewhat circular, to say the least. Furthermore, that the foundational consensus rests upon "progressive states" sets off an alarm bell, to the extent that it resonates as an avatar of the concert of civilised nations, or (on the private side) the liberal community of merchants, in whose names various violations of the general interest, public order, global commons or more, have been and still are committed.

Qualification of the challenge: imagined communities. However, the point here is none of the above, but rather the way in which Gaillard's argument naturalises (makes natural-seeming) the idea of an arbitral legal order (and indeed its supportive community of progressive sovereigns) to the point that it has become unassailable as a myth or fetiche [24]. A first qualification is in order at this point. There is nothing unusual or incongruous about the discursive and semiotic processes that accompany the foundation of a legal-political order. Genealogical (rather than historical) analyses tell us that every would-be normative community rests on a story of origin, that is, cultivates a selective imaginary as to its own past through a foundational myth [25]. The most successful (in terms of persuasive efficiency and implementation) invention of (Western) modernity is (arguably at least) the sovereign

22. *Ibid.*, para. 62.
23. See again *ibid.*, para. 40, cited above.
24. A myth is a story that cannot be falsified in rational terms: see A. Hassani, *La neutralité de l'arbitrage international: essai de déconstruction d'un mythe*, PhD dissertation, Sciences Po Law School, 2021.
25. On Foucault's genealogical analysis transposed to the international legal field, see A. Rasulov, "New Approaches to International Law: Images of a Genealogy", in J. M. Beneyto and D. Kennedy (eds.), *New Approaches to International Law: The European and the American Experiences*, TMC Asser-Springer, 2012, pp. 151-191.

state itself. Its sway, hegemony, or influence upon our ways of thought, is consolidated in political terms by the "imagined" national community of which it is thought to be the legal form. As Benedict Andersen explains in this regard, the building of the collective imaginary of the (late) modern nation emerged incrementally from all the attributes and artefacts – anthems, flags, armies, constitutions, legal tradition, patriotic poetry, political discourses, literary culture, history and geography books, bureaucracies, museums and coloured maps – that lead vast numbers of people who do not know each other (and who may well have radically divergent interests and beliefs) to be ready to die for a concept [26].

Futhermore: legal fictions. If we move from political imaginaries to legal fictions, we also know that law is essentially form-giving [27] and the means by which stories about ourselves are given performative shape. In the Western tradition, (Roman) law first emerged among other belief-systems as "the mother of all fictions" [28]. In the course of the history of modernity, statehood appeared as a juridical form as powerful as property, with which it constituted both dominium and imperium, public and private empire. This law-based paradigm (often called Westphalian) mingled state and nation. In the same way that the existence of the nation is taken for granted, much of the world cannot imagine what life would be like without the state. All this means is that the (more recent) attempt to make room for a parallel arbitral order is no more and no less fictional than the creation of state law, and is equally dependent upon an imagined community [29].

The sociology of arbitration. Now Gaillard himself was surely aware of the social processes of community-building. Moreover, remarkably, he himself alerted us to the sirens of the *"force d'évocation"* of images [30].

26. B. Anderson *Imagined Communities*: *Reflections on the Origin and Spread of Nationalism*, Verso, revised ed. 2006 (opposing the nation-state as opposed to the divine or the dynastic model). On the very late historical appearance and fulfilment of the fantasy of the modern nation-state, see H. Brunkhorst, *Critical Theory of Legal Revolutions: Evolutionary Perspectives*, Bloomsbury, 2014.

27. A. Pottage, "Introduction: The Fabrication of Persons and Things", in A. Pottage and M. Mundy, *Law, Anthropology and the Constitution of the Social*, Cambridge Univ. Press, 2004.

28. Y. Thomas, "*Fictio legis*: L'empire de la fiction romaine et ses limites médiévales", (1995), 21 *Droits* 17; if aesthetics is "signature", then law is the mother of all signatures, G. Agamben, *The Signature of All Things: On Method,* Zone books, New York, 2008, p. 33 ss.

29. For an ontological approach to the social groups or communities that participate in transnational private economy, see T. Fisher, "Nomos without Narrative", *Theoretical Inquiries in Law*, 9.2 (2008).

30. *Ibid.*, para. 6.

His own further contribution to the sociology of arbitration [31] is not only that it provides a precious view from the inside, but also that it rests, as one critic has acknowledged, on a solid reading of Bourdieu [32]. However, it is also noteworthy that the incisive edge of Garth and Dezalay's sociological-legal study – in the tradition of which Gaillard locates his own work – has become blunted to the point that the self-referentiality of arbitral doctrines has become a positive value and not a potential source of (political or gender) bias or (intellectual or ethical) closure though expertal empowerment. The industry has acquired prestigious academic credentials and produces its own reviews, colloquia and events. As empirical studies show, doctrines embedded in an unofficial form of arbitral case-law that produces an appearance of natural-seeming consistency emerge from a very small archive of decisions; many arbitrators cross-refer back to cases that are re-used to consolidate future moves [33]. That such a phenomenon is identical to the creation of case-law in state legal systems may be entirely accurate, but is also beside the point. There is nothing natural about the coherence of the collective normative narrative produced thereby.

The core problem: naturalisation. The argument here is not that fictions and imaginaries permeate the law but that these processes of self-referentiality are occulted and embedded in ways that exclude power structures from the equation [34]. Critical legal thought in other fields has taught us to be wary of the ways in which naturalisation shuts off alternatives, making us accept unquestioningly a state of affairs that is in reality contestable and highly political [35]. In this respect, there is a striking consensus among all those who purport to be part of an epistemic arbitral community not only on a clearly well-intentioned commitment to transnational justice, but also with regard to a certain number of normative principles, often characteristic of more traditional

31. See his "Sociology of International Arbitration" (2015), 31 *Arbitration International* 1. This work is by way of a (somewhat ambivalent) response to Y. Dezalay and B. Garth's canonical, *Dealing in Virtue*, Chicago Univ. Press, 1996.

32. R. Keucheyan, "Un intellectuel discret au service du capital. A la recherche des véritables penseurs de droite", *Revue du Crieur*, La Découverte 2016/1, n° 3, p. 132 à 149.

33. S. Puig, "Social Capital in the Arbitration Market", *Eur. Journ. Int. Law*, 2014, 25-2.

34. This is of course true too for the sovereign nation-state, on the foundational void of which, see E. Santner, *The Royal Remains – The People's Two Bodies and the Endgames of Sovereignty*, Chicago Univ. Press, 2011.

35. That the contention in respect of the foundations of an arbitral order is just that, is a point to which we shall return below.

forms of legal consciousness in private law [36]. For example, the myth of neutrality, hotly contested in respect of the latter [37], holds its discursive own here: commercial international arbitration is presented as the optimal if not the only way to escape the possible partiality of state courts. The net outcome of discursive naturalisation processes has been to ward off critique. Such a defensive move usually takes refuge in the seemingly self-evident superiority (impartiality, neutrality, efficiency) of inside expertise [38].

What of the lag? By contrast, outside arbitration, at least some ground has been conceded to issues of power, even in private law (that could be considered as neoliberalism's preferred playground [39]). Often, contestation has seeped through (albeit in fainter versions) from public law, where it has taken hold in constitutional issues such as discrimination or systemic bias in respect of race, gender or sexual orientation, or the social and distributional consequences of institutions. Such a lag, or (commercial) arbitration's notably immunity from critique, may only be a question of time, since we are discussing a would-be legal order that despite its own genealogical claims, is certainly less venerable than that of international or domestic nation-state. Yet, the "intimations" of the somewhat analogous aspirational non-state "global" legal order [40] are

36. For evidence of this proximity, see for example The Right Hon. The Lord Thomas of Cwmgiedd, Lord Chief Justice of England and Wales, "Developing commercial law through the courts: rebalancing the relationship between the courts and arbitration", The Bailii Lecture, 2016.

37. A. Hassani, *op. cit.*

38. This rhetoric was very present in defence of arbitration at the time of the negotiation of the transAtlantic trade and investment treaty (notably in the context of the EU Commission's public consultation: https://eur-lex.europa.eu/legal-content/EN/TXT/PDF/). For an example of the latter, see for example M. Sornarajah, "An International Investment Court: Panacea or Purgatory?" Columbia FDI Perspectives Perspectives on topical foreign direct investment issues, No. 180, 15 August 2016). Another example of such a defence can be found in E. Gaillard's own case-note under the Achmea case (CJUE 6 mars 2018, aff. C-284/16, *Revue critique de droit international privé*, 2018 p. 616. "L'affaire *Achmea* ou les conflits de logiques"), suggesting that objections to arbitration emanate from those who are on the outside and do not understand. A further French commentary on the current case law of the ECJ that was published at the very time the present text was written, describes the ECJ's position as "acrimonious towards arbitration" and announces terrifying consequences: un arrêt *London Steam-Ship* de la Cour de justice (CJUE, 20 juin 2022, aff. C-700/20), par lequel la Cour de justice de l'Union européenne (CJUE) révèle que son acrimonie à l'encontre de l'arbitrage n'est pas limitée au droit des investissements. Elle concerne désormais l'arbitrage commercial et c'est tout l'édifice qui se met à trembler (Chronicle by J. Jourdan-Marques, Actualité Dalloz, 13 July 2022).

39. See H. Brabazon, *op cit.* This does not mean of course that neoliberalism can't be constitutionalised, see H. Alviar and G. Frankenberg, *Authoritarian Constitutionalism: Comparative Analysis and Critique*, Elgar, 2019. But this is quite another issue!

40. N. Walker, *Intimations of Global Law*, CUP, 2016.

subjected to very searching scrutiny [41] and would seem to point to the fact that opening up to discussion could provide a source of legitimacy for the arbitral order itself.

41. See for example, M. Xifaras, *op. cit.*

CHAPTER II

EPISTEMOLOGY: THE MISSING IMPLICATIONS OF LEGAL PLURALISM

You cannot be a selective legal pluralist. One of the registers on which such scrutiny should occur relates to the relationship between the would-be "arbitral legal order" itself and a wider epistemological framework. In other words, by claiming that a corpus of practices, texts and decisions constitutes a form of self-standing non-state-law, independently of any delegation of normative authority by any one sovereign, Gaillard subscribes to a legal pluralist paradigm. In concrete terms, the latter involves the status of arbitral awards before state courts, but must in all coherence also relate, reciprocally or symmetrically, to the status before both state courts and arbitrators themselves of all sorts of exogenous normativities. In other words, you cannot be a selective pluralist. If you accept that something other than state norms fulfil the conditions that define law, then all norms that fit this definition must be considered as such. Any selection thereafter in respect of such claims will be related to the political or ethical acceptability of foreign norms and must be located on the register of public policy.

Bracketing the definition of legality. At this stage, we have to bracket the vast philosophical question of what defines legality. Most arbitration doctrines tend to be satisfied with the largely organic criterion delivered many decades ago in the context of the *lex mercatoria* debate (mentioned above). A set of norms is a legal order when it comprises the means to ensure its own adaptation, evolution and survival. While this definition certainly does the job for the *lex mercatoria*, and puts arbitral jurisdiction in a central place, it carries implications that reach far beyond this context. Of course, as is often said in discussions on legal pluralism, law has to draw the line somewhere [42]. Indeed, under some analyses in comparative legal epistemology, legality itself is a repeated exercise in dichotomic line-drawing. But unless we subscribe to the idea that there is an unwritten truth hidden somewhere in the law's own constitution that contains the key to

42. N. Roughan and A. Halpin, *In Pursuit of a Pluralist Jurisprudence*, CUP 2015, wondering whether a pluralist legal paradigm has to include bus queues and tea ceremonies.

its essence (although still remains to be discovered after centuries of monkish textualisms, legal positivisms, judicial originalisms or sociological analyses), law's own frontiers are variously drawn in the wake or mirror of properly philosophical-ethical and political-economic ideas, that call in turn for exploration. We shall come back to this point again below.

Legal pluralism v. *value pluralism*; *freedom* v. *autonomy*. Of more immediate relevance here is a distinction implicit in Gaillard's claim, between legal and value pluralism, or between liberal freedoms and the recognition of plural forms of legality. His ambition is not to found an arbitral order on a mere concession by a liberal state to pockets (or facts) of foreign normative practices, in the name of individual (say, contractual) freedom. Such a hypothesis would still belong to the (rejected) Westphalian model, because it implies that the state has a monopoly on legality (although of course, it is free to outsource its production, for instance to custom or to foreign law). We can see the difference very distinctly in current debates in Western polities about the status of religious awards or decisions, particularly in the field of family law. The issue in this context is the extent to which (say) the claim of a religious community to live under its own rules can be accommodated within the framework of religious freedom constitutionally guaranteed by the host territorial state, or whether such rules are an autonomous legal system, implemented, interpreted and applied by its own tribunals. The great "shariah law row" in the United Kingdom a decade ago stemmed from the suggestion by the Archbishop of Canterbury that Muslim communities ought to be able to live under their own codes (except in the field of public and criminal law)[43]. In turn, the ECtHR stopped short of allowing *Refah Partisi* to incarnate more than religious freedom in Turkey: while value pluralism was central to democracy, legal pluralism was beyond the pale [44].

Legal monism and foreign law. However, the objections to the latter were based on the state's prescriptive monopoly, even if the state is liberal in the sense that it can allow in exogenous norms by delegation (as seen above), which in turn presupposes that the latter are (otherwise) mere fact. This is what legal monism, linked historically to

43. For Archbishop Rowan Williams's plea for greater legal pluralism, see https://www.independent.co.uk/news/uk/home-news/archbishop-ignites-sharia-law-row-779505.html.

44. ECtHR *Refah Partisi (the Welfare Party) and Others* v. *Turkey [GC]* -. 41340/98, 41342/98, 41343/98 *et al.*, Judgement 13 February 2003 [GC].

the Westphalian paradigm, actually does in respect of foreign law. As every private international lawyer knows, the effect of the territorial sovereign's prescriptive monopoly is to put in place a frontier control over exogeneous normativities; if not made or adopted or vetted or incorporated or delegated by the sovereign, these simply do not count as law. Of course, over the centuries, there are multiple inconsistencies that weaken the fence and the defence. The status of foreign law is a case in point since its factual status in procedural terms before an exogenous forum does not prevent its being acknowledged by the latter as prescriptive in its own jurisdiction: indeed such acknowledgement is the very reason for which it is deemed applicable. Moreover, territory disappeared long ago in favour of more metaphysical or metaphorical conceptions of spatiality, that in turn tend to displace the centre of gravity of the Westphalian model [45].

All manner of belief systems. All this leads back to the point made above. Far beyond the old *lex mercatoria* hypothesis, if there exists such a thing as law beyond the state (a thesis to which I subscribe, normatively) then it must include everything that either corresponds to an (unlikely) universally accepted ontological definition or it must include everything that claims to be such. Hence the recurring legal pluralist dilemma: "does anything go"? The idea of a claim or a self-definition, as a key to legal pluralism, is suggested in legal-sociological theory [46] and – a key point for private international lawyers – in the constitution of statutist theories of the conflict of laws. Without any further exploration of this philosophical dilemma, it seems to me that if arbitration awards emanate from an autonomous self-standing legal order, in such a way that they escape what R. Wai' terms "jurisdictional touchdown" [47] then potentially, decisions, rulings and other normative enunciations emitted by all manner of belief systems must also be law. To be fully pluralist – that is, to claim legal status for private arbitral awards – means that the arbitrator must also make way for exogenous normativities, whether state-based or pertaining to these other communities with their specific ontologies and their own claims

45. As Gaillard's grid shows: the focus on enforcement corresponds to his second model.

46. On the idea of the claim as focus of a pluralist analysis, see R. Cotterrell and M. del Mar (eds.), *Authority in Transnational Legal Theory Theorising Across Disciplines, Elgar Studies in Legal Theory*, Elgar, 2016.

47. R. Wai, "Transnational Liftoff and Juridical Touchdown: The Regulatory Function of Private International Law in an Era of Globalization" (2002), 40 *Columbia Journal of Transnational Law*, 209.

to autonomy of governance. In other words, "intégrer le point de vue des arbitres" by state courts has to imply the reverse and indeed to extend to all the others [48].

Example: indigenous cosmologies. The most obvious examples of the latter are varieties of indigenous cosmologies still resisting extinction within the confines of the modern territorial state, or again, the codes of religious communities. This seems far from current arbitral practice, which tends to adopt a largely exclusionary stance in respect of positions or claims that do not fit a classical liberal contract-and-property-based paradigm – even when such a stance is grounded discursively on the autonomy of the arbitral legal order! It may be of course that most cosmological or religious claims [49] tend to surface in the distinct context of investment arbitration, in the form of alternative modes of non proprietorial relationships to sacred land, in conflict with modern modes of acquisition of private property [50]. Indeed, disputes between businesses do not generally involve parties other than corporations or trusts.

Future mutations. However, it is already predictable that the very structure of legal process as forged within classical adjudication will be seen as too narrow [51]. This is true for adversarial trials in state courts, which provides the model for standard arbitration procedure. As we know, multiple interests are beginning to claim legal agency – hence the appearance of unfamiliar entities such as rivers, cultural objects, the ghosts of the historically wronged, or future generations. In the era of the post, the neo and the ecological, it is likely that jurisdictional conflicts (like the conflict of laws) will become far more complex in both pragmatic and philosophical terms. In such a context, it is foreseeable (and desirable) that Gaia, who points (in Latour's terms [52]) towards an "ecological jurisprudence" will enjoin us to undertake a conceptual overhaul in respect of foundational monist concepts, including title

48. "Aspects philosophiques", para. 41.

49. The famous *Jivraj* case in the UK (*Jivraj* v. *Hashwani* [2011] UKSC 40) transformed an initially religious telos into a secular juridical debate about the legal status of arbitrators and the scope of discrimination law.

50. For examples, see S. Brachotte, *The Conflict of Laws and Non-Secular Worldviews: A Proposal for Inclusion*, Doctoral Dissertation, Sciences Po, Law School, defended May 2022, showing however that state courts do not do much better. . .

51. For an early discussion on an analogous point, see W. M. Weidermaier, "Arbitration and the Individuation Critique", *Arizona Law Rev.* (2007), Vol. 40.69.

52. For example, see the striking series of contributions in B. Latour *et al.*, *The Book of the Body Politic. Connecting Biology, Politics and Social Theory*, Fondazione Cine 2017.

(whether private property or sovereign dominium), consent (whether social or private contract) but also the distinction between persons and things (that is the juridical form of the divide between nature and culture). For Latour, non-state (indeed non-human) constituencies or bodies politic may secrete their own legal orders. To come back down to Earth (again Latour's words), the (less ambitious) point here is if arbitration has a philosophy, then it cannot allow awards to accede to autonomous legal status before state courts and then refuse an analogous status to other belief-systems before arbitrators [53].

53. On arbitrators "reluctance" to varying degrees to see such cosmologies as "law", see for instance F. Baetens (ed.), *Investment Law within International Law. Integrationist Perspectives*, CUP, 2013, pp. 106-128.

CHAPTER III

TELOS: THE POLITICAL ECONOMY OF INTERNATIONAL ARBITRATION

Immunity from political strands of contestation. However, it seems to me that the lack of inclination of the epistemic arbitral community to envisage this reciprocal move in favour of other would-be non-state orders is not driven by philosophical concerns, but is linked to the telos of arbitration in political economic terms. Beyond the usual reluctance of legal scholarship to upset embedded epistemologies or cultural traditions, there is something about the (ethereal? conflicted?) world of international arbitration that seems to have inhibited the deployment of the requisite interdisciplinary register with which to build an alternative worldview. The field seems untouched by all the sets of critiques that would seem to be eminently relevant to it. Thus, there is little challenge (from critical legal studies) to its basic tenets of legal interpretation or the distinction between form and substance; (from political economy of capitalism) to embedded concepts of (private) law such as property or contract; (from genealogical analysis) to the power structures involved in the instituional structures; (from feminist, race and queer scholarship) to racial, gender or cultural biases; (from symmetrical anthropology) to the series of rituals, networks and myths entertained by the happy few and projected as a wide belief system with the adhesion and obedience of a massive audience. None of these strands of contestation that are active in neighbouring areas appear to have penetrated the wall purportedly made (as we have seen) of technical expertise.

The exception: investment arbitration. An important exception is of course the political-economy critique of investment arbitration, that now has a wide intellectual audience, particularly in the Global South[54]. This has seeped through from public international law because of the presence of (often poor) host states in the structural relationship underlying investment disputes, making the way notably for post-colonial critique. International commercial arbitration is curtained off

54. For leading examples M. Sornarajah, *The International Law on Foreign Investment*, Cambridge University Press, 2010; K. Miles, *The Origins of International Investment Law: Empire, Environment and the Safeguarding of Capital*, Cambridge University Press, 2013.

from the latter because it applies (purportedly) to apolitical matters between equal parties arguing about the consequences of private agreements. This distinction is as doubtful however, as the public/private distinction elsewhere in the law, including or especially in its international dimension. Without taking up this well-laboured point, it is sufficient to refer, for example, to the studies of the genealogy of investment arbitration, that show how, during the first half of the twentieth century, arbitral doctrines were incrementally laying out the (largely private law) building blocks that were to "make the world safe for investment" after the independence of the colonised world, ensuring thereby that the newfound sovereignty of the latter did not entail effective control of local natural resources [55]. Today, further blurrings come from the inclusion within the field of investment arbitration of disputes by vulture funds over sovereign debt, or the conundrum of disputes arising from global value chains as they replace more traditional patterns of markets.

Law and politics? Thereafter, one of the important discursive effects of arbitration studies is precisely to have reinforced the separation of commercial arbitration as the apolitical other of the messier world of investment treaties. While attempts – through extraordinary doctrines of state contracts or of informed consent of poor states – to depoliticize may by and large have failed, the dividing line between law and politics has become displaced. Investment may have become a political field in which struggles between the highly diverging interests of various constituencies come to a head before arbitration tribunals; but over the fence, in the juridical sphere of commercial disputes, where investment is renamed property, neutrality and legal technicality come back into their own. Such representations serve, in Sundhya Pajuhah's terms, to "capture the space of the international" [56]. We circle back here to a theme – that of the evocative power of collective representations – that is central to Gaillard's argument. In other words, "we" (modern Western lawyers with a classical legal education and mindset) believe that "real" law is properly distinct from politics. Since the Westphalian world has become one of struggle, an elevated autonomous transnational juridical

---

55. A. Leiter-Bockley, *Making the World Safe for Investment: the Protection of Foreign Property 1922-1959*, PhD, 2019, Melbourne Law School/Vienna Law School.

56. S. Pajuha, "Conserving the World's Resources?", in James Crawford and Martti Koskeniemmi (eds.), *Cambridge Companion to International Law*, Cambridge University Press, 2012.

order administered by a close-knit set of able experts appears as the best way of bringing back order to the international community.

Deeper implications. Such a discourse is uncannily familiar. It appears in analogous terms in the ideological justifications of classical legal consciousness and of course in modern public international law. The latter devised ethical-legal principles that were however singularly ineffective when it came to preventing or putting a stop to egregious exploitation of one part of the world by another. I do not have time here to undertake a "critical conversation" on law and colonial and postcolonial capitalism [57] (such a conversation having already been attempted indeed in respect of the intellectual stance of Gaillard himself, who clearly invited such controversy by venturing onto the terrain of social theory [58]) nor indeed in the ways in which, in the very same founding moments that gave form to social and political injustice, modern law has also contributed to/surfed upon the bifurcation between nature and culture that conferred upon humanity an ontological privilege over other forms of life [59]. It suffices here to recall that such deep schemes are as many ways of defining and embedding exclusionary relationships in respect of alterity. The point that I am making here is that it is important, particularly in an area of the law where the underlying economic stakes are so high, that our eyes do not remain wide shut in respect of all the social and ecological implications of apparently innocuous legal devices and, to return once again to Gaillard's own words, their underlying representations.

By way of adieu. Of course, I am not insinuating in any way that Emmanuel was not a liberal and open-minded thinker. On the contrary! As I noted at the beginning of this short lecture, he was a (rare) lawyer-intellectual, whose extraordinary success as an arbitrator lay to a large extent in the combination of dialectical talent and deep scientific

---

57. The reference is to the title of the book co-authored on capitalism by Nancy Fraser and Rahel Jaeggi, *Capitalism, A Conversation in Critical Theory*, Polity Press, 2018.

58. On the contribution of E. Gaillard (as a thinker of arbitration) to neoliberal capitalism, see R. Keuchayan, *op. cit.*, as to the role of all the "praticiens et producteurs d'idées qui se chargent de fabriquer les concepts et techniques du capitalisme mondial: l'innovation technologique, la création de produits financiers ou encore la conquête incessante de nouveaux marchés. La preuve par l'exemple avec Emmanuel Gaillard, théoricien mondialement reconnu de l'arbitrage – institution centrale du capitalisme contemporain chargée de régler les litiges entre les investisseurs privés internationaux (multinationales, hedge funds. . .) et les Etats – et lecteur de Pierre Bourdieu".

59. Ph. Descola, *Par delà de Nature et Culture*, Gallimard, Folio, 2005. The point in the text above is that this privilege is perfectly analogous to the West's self-assigned prerogative over the rest.

curiosity. On the one hand, he clearly thrived on discussion – the more polemical the better [60]. On the other hand, Emmanuel had a thirst for opening up further intellectual frontiers: let us remember that well before he explored Bourdieu, his doctoral dissertation was devoted to the study of power in private law. An appropriate topic for an arbitrator, as he would later quip! But while I like to remember him, personally, through his characteristic sense of humour, the substantive discussion above is meant as a very serious hommage to the path-breaker who accepted to open up the field to which he devoted his life and *œuvre* to deep interdisciplinary exchange and critique.

This is his legacy, to be treasured.

60. His numerous interventions on the hottest of topics bear witness to this taste for debate, and I (as many others) have many anecdotes of long conversations (and disagreements) beyond technical topics (for instance on the notion of the good life). I remember one such discussion when John Rawls came over to Paris to talk about justice, rue d'Ulm. His own thorough study of Bourdieu is a further case in point: he knew perfectly well that the use he made of social theory would give rise to reactions by sociologists: how could it be otherwise?

EMMANUEL GAILLARD, THE POSITIVIST

by

Diego P. Fernández Arroyo *

1. The incredible number of tributes rendered across the globe following the passing of Emmanuel Gaillard confirmed the unique notoriety which he enjoyed as one of the most brilliant jurists of his generation, the rightful perception that he was an exceptionally kind and good man, not to forget and most importantly for the purpose of this contribution, the truly transnational reach of his ideas [1]. When reading such tributes, I could, however, not help but to be puzzled to encounter some misunderstanding or even misrepresentations of what I always understood to be fundamental tenets of Gaillard's praised representations of international arbitration, and which, as is well known, were presented at the Hague Academy some fifteen years ago in his celebrated course on the *Aspects philosophiques du droit de l'arbitrage international* [2]. Of course, Gaillard himself denounced the caricatures which were occasionally mockingly made of a sort of arbitration in the "transnational firmament".

2. In fact, even the proposed topic for this tribute – Emmanuel Gaillard, the positivist – was perceived by some as an interesting "provocative" title. Certainly, Emmanuel Gaillard was the last one to shy away from provocative proposals, but clearly the present tribute never aimed to uncover possibly hidden aspects of Gaillard's thinking. Its aim is much simpler; a modest attempt to recall what the father of the transnational legal arbitral order always openly acknowledged, that is to say, his self-perception as a positivist [3].

---

* Professor, Science Po Law School, Paris.

1. Emmanuel Gaillard was good, in the good sense of the word, as Antonio Machado famously said of himself in *Retrato*: "soy, en el buen sentido de la palabra, bueno". The tributes were collected and published in a book entitled *Par-delà le soleil: Emmanuel Gaillard*, Gaillard Banifatemi Shelbaya Siino (2021).

2. E. Gaillard, "Aspects philosophiques du droit de l'arbitrage international", *Recueil des cours* 329 (2007) 49. The course was afterward published in several other languages.

3. I believe it is entirely appropriate to see in Gaillard a *transnational* positivist. The qualification – which he uses in his 2007 Course – is necessary, as will be explained in this contribution, see *infra* para. 32.

3. This contribution is based on the tribute paid to Gaillard in The Hague on 5 August 2022. Rather than for me to engage in a series of simulated conversations with Gaillard – as it was my first intention – I decided to design a presentation for the students in the room, with the aim to let them discover the multifaceted person. The visual presentation accompanying the tribute included several *clins d'œil* to yet another aspect of Gaillard: an art *connoisseur* with a passion for Kandinsky who also occasionally produced a few sketches and drawings [4]. But most importantly, video extracts of Gaillard himself were included to confirm that Gaillard's self-perception as a positivist has always been an open secret [5].

4. As a starting point, it is important to focus on Gaillard's multiple facets (Chap. I) as well as his legal influences (Chap. II). This background allows to better grasp the fundamental tenets of Gaillard's conception of the law (Chap. III) which in turn help to understand the positivist nature of Gaillard's understanding of the law of arbitration (Chap. IV).

---

4. I cannot avoid to thank A. Senegacnik's artistic contribution (as Aleks) with the graphic presentation reproduced in this lecture. Even though I am the only responsible for its substantial content, the art conception – inspired by Kandinsky – comes from him, who, by the way, wrote his PhD thesis on the interpretation of investment treaties under the dual supervision of E. Gaillard and myself.

5. The present written contribution builds upon this visual presentation. Links to the videos are provided and the reader is encouraged to listen, rather than to merely read the transcribed text.

CHAPTER I

GAILLARD'S MULTIPLE FACETS

5. Much has already been written about Gaillard's multiple facets. His legal *œuvre* is a coherent and systemic one, offering a meticulous panoramic portrait of our contemporary legal landscape. Ongoing dynamics and pressures are punctiliously represented, and the most pressing challenges jurists have to face have been properly identified and signalled.

6. One should add that Gaillard's *œuvre* is truly original. I remember him as one of the rare persons who truly innovated. As the great Fritz Junger himself once told, the vast majority of discussed topics in legal scholarship have most likely already been considered and even experienced in the past, and sometimes even under the same label! Gaillard was an exception in this regard, and several of his works may properly be labelled as original. To cite only one, his contribution, together with Yas Banifatemi, on the negative effect of the *compétence compétence* principle has opened a path which is now routinely taken by lawyers, legislators, judges in their daily work [6].

7. What stands out in the vast majority of the tributes rendered to this day is this idea and image of Gaillard as a light. By this, people referred not only to his enlightening ideas, but also to the man. In French the word *rayonnant* appears the most fitting; it may be translated as shining. Meeting Gaillard always turned out to be a matchless pleasing and inspirational experience. The stellar lawyer was an ingenuously humble man, leaving hardly anyone indifferent.

8. Let me focus on the defining characteristic of his intellectual contributions – spanning over four decades – which illuminate his writing perspective. In fact, his contributions as an author were distinctively based on the combination and articulation of various perspectives. The fact that these perspectives were not always complementary, but sometimes clashing, explains the robustness of his intellectual constructions. Put simply, Gaillard's ideas were always "tried" from all these

6. E. Gaillard and Y. Banifatemi, "Negative Effect of Competence-Competence: The Rule of Priority in Favour of the Arbitrators", in E. Gaillard and D. Di Pietro (eds.), *Enforcement of Arbitration Agreements and International Arbitral Awards – The New York Convention Practice*, Cameron May (2008) 257.

perspectives. In this regard, I distinguish the change of perspectives on two planes.

9. Firstly, a cross-disciplinary plane. Many jurists excel in the art of "touching upon" multiple topics in an interdisciplinary manner. Gaillard did more than "touching upon": he built interdisciplinary bridges to connect what many regrettably still perceive as remote islands separated by seas and oceans of conceptual differences. Categorisations and delimitations were in this sense methodically questioned and dismissed for their simple lack of *raison d'être*. I may highlight in particular here again two aspects of this cross-disciplinary reach of his thinking. A first aspect is that Gaillard was among the club of select lawyers involved in the triad of private international law, arbitration and comparative law. The General Course which he was about to deliver in 2022 at the Academy was eagerly awaited [7]. His proposed "new theory of conflict of systems" – of which we regrettably have only the title – would evidently have explored again all aspects of the triad. Personally, I was particularly impatient to discover the aspects of the course devoted to the conceptualisation of private international law in our postglobal age. Private international law was always present in Gaillard's thought with a decidedly embracing scope including habitual questions of international jurisdiction, choice of law, judicial cooperation *lato sensu* and the recognition/enforcement of international decisions. In addition, Gaillard further embraced other non-litigation-oriented functions of private international law which clearly went beyond the mere selection of applicable laws [8]. And this one aspect – which I fully share [9] – is particularly relevant to understand Gaillard's conception of arbitration. In Gaillard's view, the main methodological debate of international arbitration law lies in the option between the (traditional) conflict approach and the (pragmatic) substantial approach *(méthodes des règles matérielles)*:

7. Like any other scholar interested in such evolution, he went to the essential source – may I simply say to "the" source? – which are the *Recueil des cours* of The Hague Academy. Unsurprisingly, the main foundations of his theories evidence a careful reading of The Hague lectures.

8. See J.-M. Jacquet, "La pensée d'Emmanuel Gaillard et le droit international privé", *Journal de droit international* (2022) 1181 On this point, even if under different conceptions, it is also important to consult G. A. Bermann, "International Arbitration and Private International Law", *Recueil des cours* 381 (2017) 41.

9. I agree that the purists who still think that the conflict of law approach is the ideal one for arbitration simply do not offer any real or serious argument to dismiss the option ultimately favoured by Gaillard. As Luca Radicati di Brozolo, we may just face a case of intellectual laziness, and sometimes absence of courage. (See L. Radicati di Brozolo's contribution in this volume.)

"One of the most fundamental methodological debates in arbitration law – [is] the following one. When confronted with attempts to evade the operation of an arbitration agreement or, more generally, to disrupt an ongoing arbitration, should arbitrators or courts seek to identify the law applicable to the issue at hand or should they resort to a different methodology, that of the substantive rules approach *(méthode des règles matérielles)*? So, do you want to follow a traditional choice of law approach and find the applicable law to the answer or develop rules which are specifically tailored to respond to a particular arbitration problem? And this is in my opinion, one of the – if not the – most fundamental methodological divide in contemporary arbitration and it has been for some time." [10]

A second aspect to mention is that Gaillard's cross-disciplinary reach was in no way limited to the previously mentioned triad. He was an international lawyer in the true meaning of the term, including public and private international law [11]. He openly advocated for the need to embrace public and private international law and for sure practised what he preached [12].

10. Besides the aforementioned cross-disciplinary plane, one must also imperatively recall that a distinctive characteristic of Gaillard as a man were the different facets of his rich personality. Firstly, he was a grand professor of law [13]. Secondly, he was a formidable – in the sense of fearsome, *redoutable* – counsel with one of the most impressive track records considering the incredible diversity of disputes he engaged

---

10. The extract is from his (virtual) lecture delivered for the American University Washington College of Law on "Seven Dirty Tricks in International Arbitration" which is available at https://www.youtube.com/watch?v=l8RF9Xq_MQY (last accessed on 20 August 2022).

11. On the topic, see D. P. Fernández Arroyo, "Réflexions autour du besoin réciproque entre le droit international privé et le droit international public", in *Le 90e anniversaire de Boutros Boutros-Ghali. Hommage du Curatorium à son Président*, Brill, 2012, 113.

12. Among his many positions, Gaillard was also the director of the *Journal de droit international*. Renvoi – L. Radicati di Brozolo about private international law in Gaillard's thinking.

13. He properly mastered the art of not only lecturing but most importantly stimulating his students and peers alike throughout his entire career. His dedication to teaching was boundless as perhaps best evidenced by his efforts to create the successful International Academy for Arbitration Law in Paris, under the model of The Hague Academy. When it comes to his role of doctoral supervisor, those who worked with him mentions adjectives such as patient, open-minded, inspirational, available, approachable. . .

with [14]. Thirdly, alongside his role as counsel, he acted as transnational arbitrator [15]. Lastly, as previously expected, he was also a brilliant intellectual, and in particular a true comparatist [16]. This is yet another feature which explains the richness of his scholarship as he was able to properly combine these perspectives.

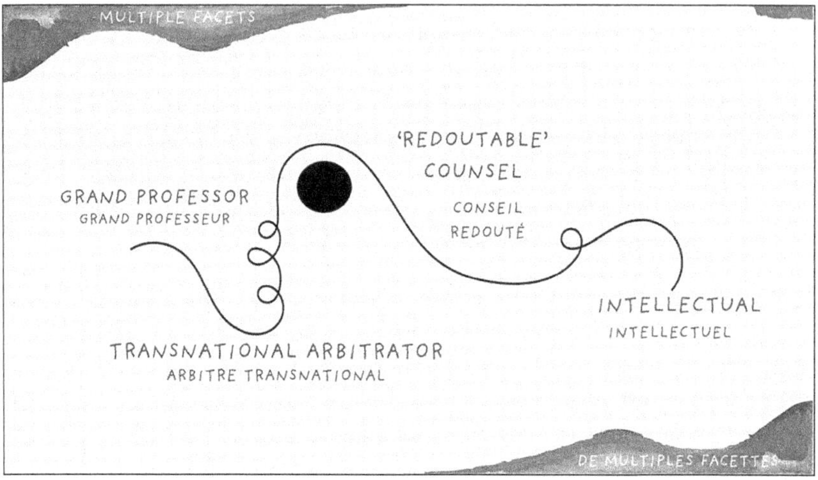

Fig 1. Gaillard's multiple facets inspired by Kandinsky's *Point and line to plane*

14. Rather than engaging in this written contribution in the futile exercise of case dropping, it must however imperatively be highlighted that here again, Emmanuel Gaillard sat also as arbitrator in a wide range of disputes and under the aegis of the most prestigious arbitral institutions across the globe. (See Y. Banifatemi's contribution in this volume.)

15. This raises the controversial double-hatting issue, so criticised and difficult to understand from an academic perspective (particularly in investment arbitration), as largely accepted by the practice. Both extremes may be seen, for example in M. Lagford, D. Behn and R. H. Lie, "The Ethics and Empirics of Double Hatting", *ESIL Reflection* 6:7 (2017). While some stress the unacceptability of potential conflicts, others highlight the intellectual enrichment produced by playing different roles. See also the Article 4 of the Draft Code of Conduct prepared by ICSID and UNCITRAL, Version Five of November 2022, https://icsid.worldbank.org/sites/default/files/WP_223_advance_copy.pdf.

16. Suffice it to say here that he was the quintessential *intellectuel de premier ordre* (or an intellectual of first rank). For sure his worldwide success as an academic and practitioner, ultimately earned him some insidious critics, which tried to disqualify him as an *intellectuel de droite*. Thus, on the reductionist basis of taking the arbitration as "a central institution of the contemporaneous capitalism", some attacked Gaillard as his most prominent figure, a true – in Gramscian terms – "organic intellectual". See R. Keucheyan, "Un intellectuel discret au service du capital. A la recherche des véritables penseurs de droite", *La Découverte – Revue du Crieur* 3 (2016-1) 132. Gaillard unsurprisingly found the proper way to respond to these attacks by engaging in an analysis of the sociological aspects of arbitration, exposing the shortcomings in the critical views expressed, as well as their hidden agenda.

CHAPTER II

GAILLARD'S LEGAL INFLUENCES

11. Every author or creator, whatever the field considered, has evidently been impacted by a variety of influences. A writer will have internalized his readings of, for instance, Borges, Tolstoi or Murakami where a painter will have been influenced by the works of Picasso, Schiele or Magritte. Sometimes, identifying these influences will not be very difficult. One may recognise after a few seconds of a new song the borrowing or sampling of a typical riff as only Hendrix knew how to perform. This is an inescapable finding from which even jurists cannot free themselves. Evidently, influences can lead to different reactions: support or approval but sometimes also rejection.

12. To understand Gaillard's self-perception as a positivist, one must likewise consider the influences to which he himself was exposed. Surely, an exhaustive mapping of all legal influences is palpably even difficult to conceive. Nevertheless, what can be done is to single out the most important influences of such perceived positivism [17].

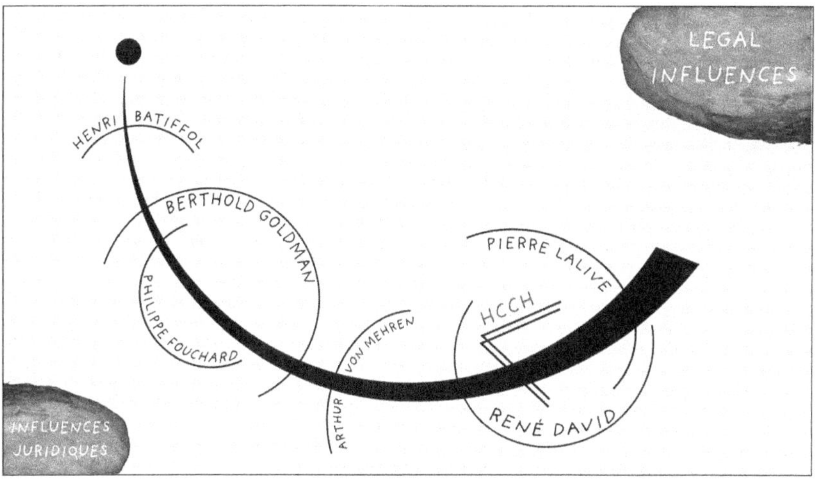

Fig 2. Gaillard's legal influences inspired by Kandinsky's
Free curve to the point

17. Surely a decisive influence for Gaillard's thinking came from his own Ph.D. supervisor, Gérard Cornu, who notably authored an innovative *Étude comparée de la responsabilité délictuelle en droit privé et en droit public*, La Mémoire du droit (1951). For sure he will have fuelled Gaillard's appetite for comparison and continuous

13. Luckily, not much effort is needed to identify such influencers and how they impacted Gaillard's legal education. In fact – surely yet another sign of his intellectual grandeur – he openly acknowledges and embraces some of his key influencers. At the beginning of his 2007 course at The Hague Academy, he pays tribute to two of his main professors at the University of Paris, none other than Henri Batiffol and Berthold Goldman.

14. Henri Batiffol was a prominent member of the Academy's Curatorium and is unanimously recognised as the leading scholar of French private international law of the last two thirds of the twentieth century [18]. His great student and later co-author Paul Lagarde, acknowledges that his mentor has been frequently and rightly considered a positivist. According to Lagarde, given the fact that the international legal order was much less developed than the national one, Batiffol "pragmatically admitted the priority of the latter" [19]. The same Lagarde, however, highlights two significant characteristics of Batiffol's scholarship: firstly, the omnipresence of a comparative dimension in his research and secondly his dissociating from nationalism which had previously inspired French leading authors such as Bartin and Niboyet. Likely, Gaillard had to intellectually "digest" – one way or another – Battifol's preference or, better priority, given in this sense to domestic law enacted by the domestic legislator and applied by the domestic judge. Gaillard's reverence for Batiffol is clearly evidenced by the very title of his 2007 course and which is an open tribute to Batiffol's *Aspects philosophiques du droit international privé* [20]. By means of his course, Gaillard tried to accomplish in the field of international arbitration what his professor had developed within the framework of private international law. Nonetheless, it is also quite evident that

exploration of public and private branches of law. One should probably also mention, another professor of the University of Paris, Bruno Oppetit, who excelled both in legal philosophy and in private international law and arbitration. See, B. Oppetit, "Philosophie de l'arbitrage commercial international", *Journal de droit international* (1993) 811, and "Le droit international privé, droit savant", *Recueil des cours* 234 (1992) 331.

18. Batiffol taught several times at the Academy. See H. Batiffol, "Les tendences doctrinales actuelles en droit international privé", *Recueil des cours* 72 (1948) 1; "Principes de droit international privé", *Recueil des cours* 97 (1959) 431; "Réflexions sur la coordination des systèmes nationaux", *Recueil des cours* 120 (1967) 9; and "Le pluralisme des méthodes en droit international privé", *Recueil des cours* 139 (1973) 75.

19. Batiffol's portrait by Paul Lagarde can be found in the *Galerie des internationalistes* of the SFDI. See https://www.sfdi.org/internationalistes/batiffol/.

20. H. Batiffol, *Aspects philosophiques du droit international privé,* Dalloz (1956).

Gaillard did not ultimately embrace Batiffol's approach, even if he perceived himself as a positivist.

15. The other person who Gaillard openly acknowledges to have had a decisive influence on his own thinking is evidently Berthold Goldman [21]. Rightfully considered to be the greatest French expert in international business law, his courses at the Academy were the seminal pieces who marked and shaped the young Gaillard [22]. Goldman's fundamental course broke the *then* mainstream doctrine by introducing a postulate which *today* appears very banal, i.e. the simple postulate that "the arbitrator has no forum". In 1963 already, Goldman accordingly wrote:

> ". . . unless we stick to the rationally unjustifiable reference to the system based on the seat of arbitration as connecting factor. . ., any search for a connecting system corresponding to the nature of international arbitration leads to the inevitable need for an autonomous system, and not a national one" [23].

16. Goldman's influence would become later a fruitful cooperation. As is well known, Gaillard would eventually publish the French leading treatise on international commercial arbitration together with another well-known disciple of Goldman, Philippe Fouchard. It is one of these very few texts entering the select club of books which are simply called by their authors' names, i.e. the *Fouchard Gaillard Goldman* [24]. With Fouchard, Gaillard shared the transnational approach towards the arbitration, as well as a critical regard on its deviations [25].

17. Yet another titan French jurist to mention is René David. As one of the most celebrated comparatists of all times, David did not only transmit to Gaillard his passion to venture outside borders, but since he also devoted a part of his impressive studies to arbitration, he provided Gaillard with often revisited sources of inspiration for his own

21. Gaillard's confirmation is not really needed inasmuch as the influence that Goldman has had on his view, and on what has ultimately become the legal theory of international arbitration presented at the Academy several decades later, is highly evident.

22. See essentially B. Goldman, "Les conflits de lois dans l'arbitrage international de droit privé", *Recueil des cours* 109 (1963) 347.

23. B. Goldman, "Les conflits de lois dans l'arbitrage international de droit privé", *Recueil des cours* 109 (1963) 379-380 (free translation).

24. *Fouchard, Gaillard, Goldman on International Commercial Arbitration*, Kluwer (1999).

25. See, for instance, Ph. Fouchard, "Anti-Suit Injunctions in International Arbitration – What Remedies?", in E. Gaillard (ed.), *Anti-Suit Injunctions in International Arbitration*, Juris (2005) 153.

thinking [26]. In his 2007 course, Gaillard makes sure to acknowledge (and reject) David's admitted preference for a jusnaturalist approach to arbitration. The "new commercial law" to be applied by arbitrators is in this perspective evidently closely related to natural law, and David himself considered that in all cases – that is to say, also when deciding as *amiable compositeur* – arbitrators should base their decisions on fairness considerations:

> "The new commercial law, as developed by corporatists arbitral tribunals is strongly influenced by natural law. Like natural law and ancient commercial law, and despite national codifications, this new commercial law is international in nature. As such, it moves away and distinguishes itself from positive national laws. Moreover, contrary to 'positive' law in various countries, it is characterized by an arbitrator's desire to take into account the commercial interests of the parties, even if that entails sacrificing, if need be, their strict rights. It is just as important to maintain good relations with one's clients or suppliers as it is to obtain what is owed to one in a given dispute." [27]

Unmistakably, David rejects any nationalist approach, and simply affirms that an international order different from the national ones exists, also within the context of private law. In David's view, the very concept of law must thus be dissociated from the idea of binding force.

18. Gaillard's legal influences are evidently not only to be found in French academic circles. In fact, in the year spent in Harvard as a young professor, Gaillard particularly engaged with Arthur von Mehren, yet another leading author in the private international law/comparative law/arbitration triad [28]. It will again come as no surprise that Gaillard's scholarship is also permeated by references to von Mehren. In fact, reciprocally, von Mehren was one of the singular American scholars who publicly praised the way in which French courts approach inter-

---

26. See, among other works, R. David, *L'arbitrage dans le commerce international*, Economica (1982), in which David supports Berthold Goldman's general understanding and intellectualisation of the *lex mercatoria*.

27. R. David, "Droit naturel et arbitrage", in *Natural Law and World Law. Essays to Commemorate the Sixtieth Birthday of Kotaro Tanaka*, Yuhikaku (1954) 24 (free translation by Gaillard).

28. T. von Mehren, "Theory and Practice of Adjudicatory Authority in Private International Law: A Comparative Study of the Doctrine, Policies and Practices of Common- and Civil-Law Systems", *Recueil des cours* 295 (1996) 9.

national arbitration[29], which, in turn, are notably influenced by the doctrine, where Gaillard's voice is singularly listened[30].

19. Later in his career, Gaillard further made no secret of his admiration for Pierre Lalive, who also excelled in the three fields of the previously mentioned triad[31]. Lalive was, just like Gaillard, one of the most famous arbitration practitioners, both as a counsel and as an arbitrator. And here again, Lalive had a defining influence on Gaillard. To take only one example, one may refer to the concept of transnational public policy or "truly international" public policy which was coined by Lalive by the end of the eighties. This concept plays a crucial role in the legal representations of arbitration, and evidently for the third representation whereby arbitrators become guardians of the arbitral legal order's transnational public policy.[32]

20. Lastly, it is also crucial not to forget the influence of his experience at the HCCH as *secrétaire-rapporteur*. Here, in The Hague, Gaillard first gained inside knowledge on the function of international organisations. He acquired the understanding of the fundamentals of the international law-making process. All who have taken part in the elaboration of international legal texts know that there is hardly any room for innovation in such fora; most solutions come from national legal systems and well-established international practices. Gaillard surely had this in mind when analysing the development of the body of rules in matter of investment law as well as the elaboration of the myriad of modern international arbitration texts by UNCITRAL. It will be no surprise that having been trained to discern and track the origin of

29. "These French developments may well constitute the most creative and probing contemporary experimentation and reflection respecting the nature of – and the characteristics required by – an effective dispute-resolution process for international commercial activities." A. T. von Mehren, "International Commercial Arbitration: The Contribution of the French Jurisprudence", *Louisiana Law Review* 46 (1986) 1059.

30. J.-P. Ancel, "Emmanuel Gaillard et la jurisprudence française en matière d'arbitrage international. Variations sur la notion d'autonomie", *Journal de droit international* (2022) 1175. See also, D. Hascher, "L'influence de la doctrine sur la jurisprudence française en matière d'arbitrage", *Revue de l'arbitrage* (2005) 391 et, du même auteur, "Les perspectives françaises sur le contrôle de la sentence internationale ou étrangère", *McGill Journal of Dispute Resolution* 1:2 (2005) 1, esp. 5. (See D. Hascher's contribution in this volume.)

31. P. Lalive, "Tendances et méthodes en droit international privé", *Recueil des cours* 155 (1977) 3.

32. See P. Lalive, "Ordre public transnational (ou réellement international) et arbitrage international", *Revue de l'arbitrage* (1986) 329. Interestingly, Lalive himself revisited the subject after reading Gaillard's 2007 Course. See P. Lalive, "L'ordre public transnational et l'arbitre international", in *Liber F. Pocar*, A. Giuffrè (2009) 599.

rules and having first-hand experience on the making of such rules, he will later embrace the third representation of arbitration and the legal arbitral order.

CHAPTER III

GAILLARD'S CONCEPTION OF LAW

21. How then did these legal influences affect Gaillard's conception of law? Surely only a first sketch of said conception can realistically be made [33]. For the purpose of this contribution, I need only to single out five defining characteristics [34].

22. A trace of the first and perhaps most important distinctive feature is to be found – among others – in a key contribution looking back at thirty years of what Gaillard himself called the "adventure" of the *lex mercatoria.* The article features a discussion of how the concept has been received as well as the backlash that it faced. On this occasion, Gaillard regrets that those approaching *lex mercatoria* as a source of law specifically designed for the business operators are prone to consider as necessary corollary the idea that domestic law would thus be unsuited:

> "By insisting on the need to identify a law adapted to the society of merchants, the expression *[lex mercatoria]* seems to postulate a contrario the inadequacy of state laws to govern international commercial relations. However, if it contains a part of truth, the idea that the specificity of international trade relations often requires its own regime, is, in this context, likely to cause some confusion. Indeed, this finding does not necessarily lead to the conclusion that it is appropriate to use standards from an international source to meet the specific needs of international trade. Each legal order can be perfectly aware of these needs and

---

33. There would be many additional features to highlight to better understand how Gaillard approached the very concept of law: law as a political product, susceptible of many abuses, and the corresponding need to be able to respond appropriately to prevent such abuse. Another feature evidently is his characteristic openness towards other social sciences and the wish to connect law with the latter as he has done for philosophy and sociology. In the introduction to his article on the sociology of arbitration, Gaillard signals that for now, sociology would be his topic of interest. He mentions that a study of the psychology of arbitration remained to be done, and that it would probably include a chapter on arbitral narcissism. For sure I would have enjoyed reading his take on this very topic. See E. Gaillard, "Sociology of International Arbitration", *Arbitration International* 31 (2015) 1.

34. From the methodological point of view, it may be highlighted that such conceptions can evidently be found in most of his works, albeit in different degrees.

> satisfy them itself by subjecting international relations to material rules different from those which govern internal relations." [35]

This extract flawlessly captures the first fundamental aspect of Gaillard's conception of law which is crucial to appreciate his self-perception as a positivist, i.e. an openness towards the application of law and certainly no discrimination against domestic law. In his *Aspects philosophiques*, Gaillard clearly highlights that his preferred third representation is "far from stigmatizing the alleged inadequacy of national laws" [36].

23. Secondly, and evidently linked to the previous article, is his embracing of *lex mercatoria* as a legal method. In this sense, Gaillard's own conception favours a different wording which is the notion of transnational rules or general principles [37]. In doing so, Gaillard proposes a dynamic methodology [38] which ultimately requires arbitrators to engage in a continuous assessment and reassessment of trade usages, practices and legal principles:

> "Contrary to the concept of lex mercatoria, which seems to postulate the specificity of transnational norms, the notion of transnational rules or general principles suggests that these norms are based on the state legal orders with which they are not in conflict but with which they maintain filial ties. The idea is no longer that of the opposition of state legal orders and a hypothetical transnational legal order but that of a global recourse to a set of national laws whose fruitfulness is thus recognized. In other words, the postulate of the inadequacy of national laws gives way to the more legitimate concern of basing the solution of certain disputes on a set of rights rather than on a single one, the original

35. E. Gaillard, "Trente ans de *lex mercatoria*: Pour une application sélective de la méthode des principes généraux du droit", *Journal du droit international* (1995) 5, at para. 4 (free translation).

36. E. Gaillard, "Aspects philosophiques du droit de l'arbitrage international", *Recueil des cours* 329 (2007) 49 at para. 53.

37. See on the distinction between usages and transnational rules and general principles, E. Gaillard, "La distinction des principes généraux du droit et des usages du commerce international", in *Etudes offertes à Pierre Bellet,* Litec (1991) 203.

38. It is a radical change of perspective to accept to see the body of rules developed over several decades one key characteristic of which is to escape from the empire of national or international law as far as both their formation and application are concerned. In this case, far from the traditional modes of thinking of private international lawyers, the transnationalist stops thinking in terms of conflict of law and territoriality and starts developing new ways of reasoning. See the description in this sense by A. Pellet, "La *lex mercatoria*, 'tiers ordre juridique'? Remarques ingénues d'un internationaliste de droit public", in *Mélanges en l'honneur de Philippe Kahn*, Litec (2000) 58.

solutions of which could disappoint the legitimate expectation of the parties." [39]

24. Thirdly, having embarked on the methodological path opened by Gaillard, it is vital to investigate the threshold which needs to be met for such transnational rule to emerge. In the Gaillardian understanding, there can simply not exist any requirement that the rule in question be unanimously accepted for it to become a transnational rule and ultimately be applied by international arbitrators. By contrast, Gaillard advocates for the majoritarian principle [40]. He for instance notoriously criticized his esteemed colleague Pierre Mayer for having concluded in his 1989 Hague Course [41] that the rule of the separability of the arbitration agreement would not constitute a general principle of arbitration law due to the *then* singular hostile position of English law (such odd solution of English Law was abandoned since the enactment of the 1996 Arbitration Act, though its current understanding is still peculiar):

> "If it were to prevail, this conception would justify all the fears with regard to transnational rules. The requirement of unanimity, or at least the veto granted to the supposedly 'most advanced' legal systems – not to mention all the risks that this notion, a cousin of the theory of lacunas, entails – would considerably reduce the interest of such method and would cast doubt on its neutrality. Why resort to the method of general principles to identify rules that are ultimately found in all legal systems?" [42]

25. Fourthly, it is necessary to consider the specific vocabulary employed by Gaillard in as much as he refers to *transnational* rather than

39. E. Gaillard, "Trente ans de *lex mercatoria*: Pour une application sélective de la méthode des principes généraux du droit", *Journal du droit international* (1995) 5 at para. 4 (free translation).

40. E. Gaillard, "Aspects philosophiques du droit de l'arbitrage international", *Recueil des cours* 329 (2007) 49, at para. 54. See also, E. Gaillard, "Transnational Law: A Legal System or a Method of Decision Making?", *Arbitration International* (2001) 61.

41. P. Mayer, "L'autonomie de l'arbitre international dans l'appréciation de sa propre competence", *Recueil des cours* 217 (1989) 319, at 432: ". . . même si le droit anglais paraît relativement isolé dans son refus, le fait qu'il constitue l'un des systèmes juridiques les plus évolués, joint à l'importance de l'Angleterre comme place d'arbitrage international (au moins dans certains domaines), exclut le consensus sans lequel un principe général du droit ne peut être constaté".

42. E. Gaillard, "Trente ans de *lex mercatoria*: Pour une application sélective de la méthode des principes généraux du droit", *Journal du droit international* (1995) 5, at para. 34 (free translation).

international rules. Admittedly, this is one element of his scholarship in which sometimes mixed signals may be perceived; Gaillard's magnum opus is, after all, entitled in English *Legal theory of international arbitration*, and not "transnational arbitration". He generally refers to transnational public policy or "truly international public policy" [43]. Does that mean that transnational can always be equated with international? I believe the answer is definitely no. What is clear to me, is that Gaillard insists on the need to accept the existence of a transnational level of normativity, distinct from the classical public international level. In this sense, he clearly presents transnational public policy as the counterpart in the field of international transactions of the international law notion of *jus cogens* [44].

26. A fifth distinctive characteristic of Gaillard's understanding of the law is contextual in nature. Put simply, Gaillard approached the law through comparative lenses. He advocated for comparative law as part of the teaching and his own works evidence the extent to which a comparative perspective as simply indispensable. His *œuvre* repeatedly discusses the many functions which comparative law may enjoy in the context of transnational arbitration. In the Gaillardian view, the comparative law analysis plays four significant roles: first, as second nature for arbitrators; second, as a source of inspiration for lawmakers; third, as a practical tool for litigants; and fourth, as a source of law in its own right [45]. Comparative law is, thus, an indispensable ingredient to fuel Gaillard's methodological enterprise to identify and eventually apply transnational rules.

27. Sixthly, and certainly not less importantly, I feel the need to add Gaillard's prescription of a certain level of chaos as a desirable feature for the proper evolution and functioning of a systemic enterprise such as

---

43. E. Gaillard, "Aspects philosophiques du droit de l'arbitrage international", *Recueil des cours* 329 (2007) 49, at para. 54.

44. See in particular, E. Gaillard, "The emergence of transnational responses to corruption in international arbitration", *Arbitration International* (2019) 1. See also, E. Gaillard, "Aspects philosophiques du droit de l'arbitrage international", *Recueil des cours* 329 (2007) 49, at para. 61.

45. Gaillard had kindly accepted the International Academy of Comparative Law's invitation to deliver the inaugural lecture of the first open access volume *Ius Comparatum* on International Arbitration and the Methodology of Comparative law. See E. Gaillard, "Comparative Law in International Arbitration".*Ius Comparatum* 1 (2020), available on https://aidc-iacl.org/journal/wp-content/uploads/sites/7/2020/11/IUS-COMPARATUM-VOL-1-2.-GAILLARD-1.pdf. See D. P. Fernández Arroyo, "Emmanuel Gaillard, le rayonnement transnational d'une pensée comparatiste", *Journal de droit international* (2022) 1193.

arbitration [46]. Such chaotical panorama is envisaged by Gaillard inside and outside the specific institutional arbitration framework, which he knew and described as no other specialist [47].

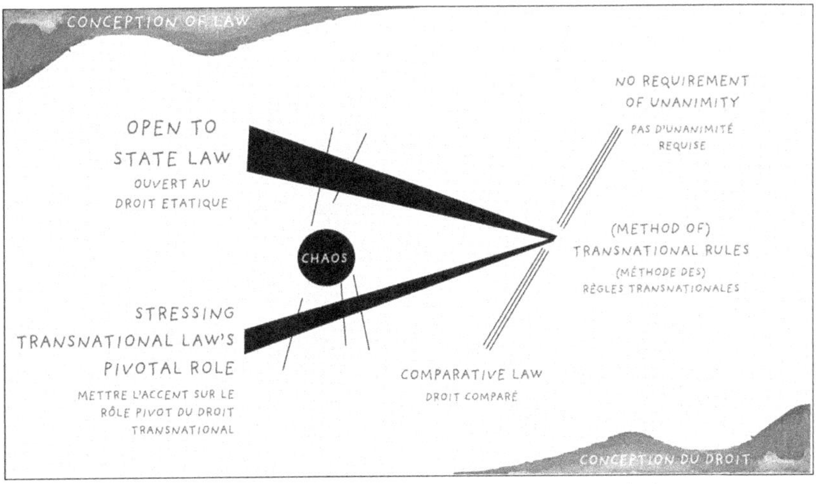

Fig. 3. Gaillard's conception of law inspired by Kandinsky's *Point and line to plane*

28. A last point had to be made for the students gathered in the auditorium of the Academy, in the form of an advice provided by Gaillard himself to the younger generations of jurists interested in building a career in arbitration [48]. In fact, while it should strictly speaking not be presented as a distinctive feature of Gaillard's own conception of law, it certainly is linked to it:

> "Arbitration is very broad. To be an arbitrator, to do arbitration is good but you also want to be a good lawyer in one legal system and also specialise in other disciplines. You want to be a great expert in M&A, in construction, in public international law. It's not so much arbitration, it's arbitration as a specific field and also,

46. E. Gaillard, "Lalive Lecture – The Myth of Harmony in International Law", *ICSID Review* 34 (2019) 553.
47. E. Gaillard, "Sociology of International Arbitration", *Arbitration International* 31 (2015) 1, spec. at 3-10 (dealing with "international arbitration as a social field"). See however, A. Mourre, "La légitimité de l'arbitrage", *Recueil des cours* 427 (2022) 211, at 255-256.
48. Gaillard had very kindly accepted to record an interview so that my students could benefit from his view even where we were not allowed to meet in class due to the pandemic.

it's also true that you can do something else. Just doing arbitration is just like doing comparative law without doing any in-depth study of any legal systems." [49]

49. See the full interview of Gaillard for Sciences Po Law School at https://www.youtube.com/watch?v=DqYfitByE1k.

CHAPTER IV

THE POSITIVISM IN GAILLARD'S CONCEPTION OF ARBITRATION

29. The fundamental question to ask before turning to Gaillard's conception of positivism, is what is after all legal positivism? An acceptable starting point is, however, a general understanding that legal positivism is based on a belief that the only legitimate source of law are the rules of law – I take the concept here in the largest possible understanding – that have been expressly recognised, promulgated or adopted by a governmental or political entity [50].

30. Obviously, there are many proud positivists with different definitional claims as to what positivism ultimately entails, e.g. from Austin to Bentham over to Kelsen and not forgetting Hart. The spectrum is quite broad but for the purpose of this contribution, it is sufficient to have a look at the extremes of the spectrum. I refer in this regard, at the one end, to State centred positivists, who will only accept the application of State made and State sanctioned law. Proponents of such State centred positivism will typically reject the application of transnational rules and the notion of arbitral legal order in the Gaillardian understanding. At the other end, one will encounter proponents of what may be labelled a transnational positivism, and to which we may precisely count Gaillard. Now, what exactly differentiates Gaillard from the other positivists, but still allows to see in him a positivist? Answering these questions requires to recall that the third representation of international arbitration itself developed into two different trends.

31. Here one will find on the one side jusnaturalists like David and Oppetit and, on the other hand, those who by contrast may be labelled as the transnational positivists. Gaillard very clearly rejects the natural law perspective as he does not find sufficient to ground the source of arbitration in higher values which are – simply put – considered

50. On the point in this regard is the following quote to be found in the relevant entry in the *Stanford Encyclopedia of Philosophy* as follows "According to positivism, law is a matter of what has been posited (ordered, decided, practiced, tolerated, etc.); as we might say in a more modern idiom, positivism is the view that law is a social construction".

to result from the nature of things or society [51]. Pursuant to the jusnaturalist trend, the arbitral legal order is understood as a collection of pre-existing rules whose source is wholly extraneous to national laws [52]. Gaillard also differentiates himself from those who, without claiming to be jusnaturalists, take moral values as a supreme reference [53].

32. In this sense and by contrast, Gaillard is definitely a transnational positivist as he grounds the arbitral phenomenon on the normative activity of States:

> "The representation that accepts the existence of an arbitral legal order . . . relies on the notion that the laws of various States, when considered collectively, make up the common rules of arbitration law in which the source of the arbitrators' power to adjudicate is rooted. Like general principles of law, which constitute one of the sources of international law, this representation is not defined in opposition to national laws. Rather, it is entirely based on the normative activity of States." [54]

33. What Gaillard ultimately does and calls for, is to contemplate the States collectively, as opposed to individually. The core of this conception was in fact the result of decades of deep reflection which can already be found in the *Fouchard Gaillard Goldman*:

> ". . . the binding effect of an award – and hence the source of the arbitrators' powers – derives from the community of legal orders which, under certain conditions, are prepared to recognize and enforce their awards in their respective jurisdictions" [55].

34. It is the vast number of States which gives to the award – and to the arbitration agreement on which it is based – its validity and ultimately its very legitimacy. Gaillard's representation corresponds to

51. E. Gaillard, "Aspects philosophiques du droit de l'arbitrage international", *Recueil des cours* 329 (2007) 49, at para. 48.

52. *Ibid.*, at para. 50.

53. *Ibid.*, at para. 49, referring to P. Mayer, "La règle morale dans l'arbitrage international", in *Etudes offertes à Pierre Bellet*.Litec (1991) 379). On this approach, from a perspective non focused on arbitration, see I. Tourkochoriti, "Beyond Legal Positivism in Transnational Law", in L. Siliquini, Cinelli (ed.), *Legal Positivism in a Global and Transnational Age*, Springer (2019) 253.

54. E. Gaillard, "Aspects philosophiques du droit de l'arbitrage international", *Recueil des cours* 329 (2007) 49, at para. 53.

55. *Fouchard, Gaillard, Goldman on International Commercial Arbitration*, Kluwer (1999) 3.

the inherent perception that transnational arbitrators do not administer justice on behalf of any given State, but that they nonetheless play a judicial role for the benefit of the transnational community[56].

35. To this day, I still have failed to encounter any justification as to why an arbitrator should render justice any differently on a Tuesday morning, deliberating as a member of an arbitral tribunal seated in Geneva, as opposed to a Tuesday afternoon, this time deliberating as a member of another arbitral tribunal seated in Mexico. In fact, precisely the very reason why this would just even be materially and physically possible is precisely because both deliberations could conveniently take place in Paris, regardless of the legal seat. In reality, and oftentimes this is the case, hearings and deliberations are conducted outside of the legal seat. Reading into the parties' choice of a seat, a wish to somehow "link" and ultimately "nationalise" their arbitration with the legal system of the seat remains in my view rather artificial[57]. Parties generally select the seat for its neutrality and arbitration friendliness. Gaillard himself criticized the "obsession" of the seat, and I could not resist sharing one of his drawings.

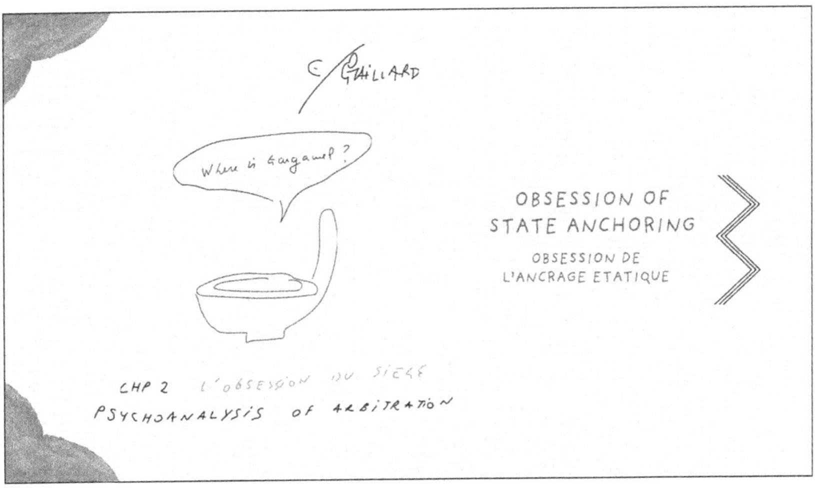

Fig. 4. The "obsession of the seat" according to Gaillard
(courtesy of Yas Banifatemi)

56. As such, the transnational arbitrator will be the guardian of said community's transnational public policy.

57. Such view is, however, still largely supported. See, for instance, Franco Ferrari, according to whom the choice of the arbitral seat identifies the *lex loci arbitri* and, thus, the applicable arbitration framework. See F. Ferrari, *"Lex Facit Arbitrum 2.0"*, *Diritto del commercio internazionale* 35 (2021) 915.

36. As Gaillard further liked to point out, strikingly the same advocates seeking to link arbitration with the legal seat and subsequently calling for a transnational effect of a setting aside decision by the seat at the same time never advocate for such transnational effect for a positive decision confirming an award [58].

37. State centred positivists will evidently find Gaillard's proposed transnational approach to be irreconcilable with their own positivistic precepts. Firstly, because the juridicity of the arbitration, even if it is grounded by Gaillard on the collective legal activity of States, is precisely not grounded on the activity of *only* one State. Certainly, if this is the defining criteria, there is not much to be done. And secondly, in all likelihood the same State-centred positivists will next object that Gaillard's proposed theory necessarily implies that the legal activity of some States may occasionally be disregarded. This is correct, particularly where such State would for instance not support the existence of a given transnational rule, or more simply where such State would not support a given arbitration proceeding or outcome, whatever the reason for this may be [59].

38. It is factually correct that Gaillard's preferred approach indeed allows to disregard an isolated perspective of a given State and there is accordingly no counter-argument to offer to the State centred positivists in this regard. Except perhaps, that such occasional disregard may be not only tolerated, but desirable. Looking at the broader picture helps to provide responsive elements to tolerate disregarding a singular State perspective. Arbitration today enjoys a quasi-exclusive jurisdiction over a still expanding scope of disputes. This is even more remarkable as arbitration is still something for which the parties effectively must opt in. The voluntary quasi-exclusive jurisdiction of arbitration disputes plainly suffices to justify the current arbitral system [60]. The legitimacy of the arbitrators' performance of her adjudicative function

58. Admittedly, the advocates of the monolocal representation of arbitration will simply counter that an annulled award simply does not exist anymore. Differently, there would be no inherent reason why an award confirmed by the jurisdictions of the seat would automatically deserve to be recognized abroad, just as is the case for any judgment rendered by the courts of the seat.

59. See *supra*, para. 24.

60. I am not prejudging that arbitration's legitimacy is guaranteed forever. Quite the contrary, and I have written elsewhere about the "price to pay" for the "arbitralization of disputes". The more disputes get submitted to arbitration, the bigger the need for arbitration to also engage in a comprehensive reform to enhance its legitimacy. See D. P. Fernández Arroyo, "Nothing is for Free: The Prices to Pay for Arbitralizing Legal Disputes", in L. Cadiet, B. Hess and M. Requejo Isidro (eds.), *Privatizing Dispute Resolution*, Nomos (2009) 615.

can hardly be disputed in the contemporary legal landscape: rather it needs to be properly acknowledged and continuously tested[61]. It is based on the consensus existing among States on this matter rather than on the specific will of given sovereign. The validity and legitimacy of the arbitral process and of the ensuing award, instead of being rooted in a single legal order, that of the seat, or, as in the second Gallardian representation, in the individual legal order of each State that may ultimately recognize the award, is found in the body of rules on which a consensus has been reached by the collectivity of States. It is premised on the simple idea that the understanding of a vast number of States must be given greater weight than that of an isolated country, be it that of the seat of the arbitration. But let Gaillard speak by himself. The following extract of a conference in Paris leaves no doubts about his view on the point:

> "First of all, I would like to say before talking about the seat and, strictly speaking, about one of the arbitration theories which explains the entire phenomenon – the one that builds all around the seat – that in the three theories that I have described in my work, none ignores the state legal orders; none is arbitration in the 'transnational firmament' as some English judges have mockingly written. Each time there are different conceptions of the relationship between arbitration and state legal orders. All three theories are positivist theories. Simply the first one says that there is a single legal order, because all this was happening in a hotel in Geneva between Swedish and Qatari parties represented by two American, English or Swiss law firms, so suddenly it becomes an arbitration which has a Swiss nationality. This is the first theory. The second is to say that there are other States which have an equal or greater title to claim or to concern themselves with the validity of an award; in the first place the State or States of recognition of this award since after all we used hotels and a Swiss stenotypist and all the others were non-Swiss personnel in my example, and if we want to enforce as a consequence that we will seize a bank account in the United States or France, perhaps the French courts of the place of enforcement, or the United States of the place of enforcement, have a stronger title to govern the phenomenon, as opposed to the State in which the material operations of the arbitration proceeding took place. This is the second conception,

61. A. Mourre, "La légitimité de l'arbitrage", *Recueil des cours* 427 (2022) 211.

the one which finally gives the place of enforcement, the State of the place of enforcement or the States of the places of enforcement, a superior right to recognize the validity of this private act which is the award and which remains private until the moment when it is given the exequatur somewhere. And in the third conception – that of the arbitral legal order – we simply go a little further and recognize that if American law, Swiss law, or French law in my previous example, have a right to concern themselves with what is a real arbitration that deserves to be recognized, there is also an activity of States, which is not only an individual activity, but which is a collective activity of States, especially in international organizations at the forefront of which the UNCITRAL: the New York Convention, the UNCITRAL model law, the Convention on transparency, there is a whole set of rules that apply to arbitration. And it is these state norms, of state origin, through which States collectively govern arbitration, and not just the rules of a random State which is the seat." [62]

62. Available on www.gbsdisputes.com (free translation).

CHAPTER V

ÉPILOGUE

39. As a result of the foregoing, I reiterate that, contrary to some wrong assumptions, the legal production of States is a central tenet in Gaillard's understand and systematisation of law. The latter is hastily if not obsessively caricatured under the heading of *denationalisation*. *Denationalisation* as a process is certainly to be distinguished from a completed stage of *denationalisation* or, in this case better, *anationalisation* [63].

40. Now what is there to say by means of conclusion of Gaillard's own perception as a positivist? He certainly claimed to be such positivist. Perhaps it is best to try to describe Gaillard's positivism, rather than to epilogue meaninglessly whether it matches this or that positivism's definition. Gaillard's positivism may be characterized as, open, transnational, progressive, pragmatic but also certainly as idealistic. Surely, I find that there is some optimism and idealism in Gaillard's preferred representation of arbitration. This is not bad in itself. I would abstain to reject a certain amount of idealism, which is always needed when dealing with legal evolution. But realistically one may also admit that Gaillard's representation presupposes certain requirements which are not going to be always (easily) met. Firstly, it will require arbitrators to live up to the role described and also prescribed by him. Practically, much help is provided today to permit gain access to arbitral decisions, and new technological tools also facilitate the transnational sharing of knowledge and legal solutions. Are arbitrators, however, all sufficiently equipped to contribute to arbitration as Gaillard envisages? Most importantly, will they be prepared to display the necessary arbitral courage to do so? Probably not, but Gaillard certainly did his utmost best to train generations of jurists to be up for the challenge. I regrettably see other obstacles on the way, which still need to be fully acknowledged and tackled. The important one which in my view deserves our attention concerns arbitral institutions. Evidently, said institutions are regularly at

63. Hence Gaillard's preference for the term transnational, by opposition to the a-national arbitral legal order of the jusnaturalists. See. E. Gaillard, "Aspects philosophiques du droit de l'arbitrage international", *Recueil des cours* 329 (2007) 49, at para. 51.

the forefront of innovation [64]. Regrettably, sometimes a policy to avoid any issues with domestic courts may also lead the same institutions to discourage, rather than encourage, arbitrators' creativity.

41. On this occasion, it should be highlighted that the series of lectures at the Academy were not merely commemorative. The current status of arbitration is certainly not immutable. Legal *status quo* is a mirage, and for generations of jurists, Gaillard was one of those at the *avant-garde* to secure and guide arbitration's propper evolution, always keeping a critical view on it and on its deviations.

42. To finish this tribute, it is appropriate to dedicate a few words to Kandinsky. As is well known, the cover of Gaillard's famous 2007 Hague Lecture represented Kandinsky's *Several circles*. The cover was evidently a conscious choice by Gaillard. For this tribute in The Hague, I decided to pick yet another picture of Kandinsky's repertoire, i.e. *The rider*. I think it provides a good closing point to think about this tension between the different positivist notions previously described. For sure, in the vision of the State centred positivist, there will always conceptually be one initial choice to make. One will always have to pick one horse to ride. In fact, in this view, there is also only "one horse" to ride at the same time which is why Gaillard's theory will fail to qualify as a positivist theory.

Fig. 5. The rider, inspired by Kandinsky's *Lyrical*

64. A particular feature, ultimately also welcomed by Gaillard, is the publication of awards. This has greatly contributed to the development of transnational rules.

43. But perhaps others will accept Gaillard's invitation to embrace what I have called a *transnational* legal positivism. A transnational legal positivism grasping the entire phenomenon of arbitration in the transnational movement of the law.

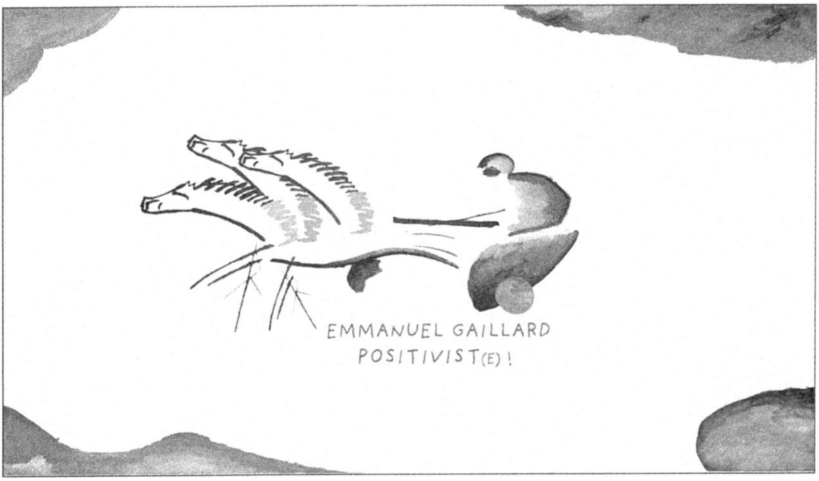

Fig. 7. The rider, also inspired by Kandinsky's *Lyrical*

UNIFORM ARBITRATION-SPECIFIC RULES *V.* DOMESTIC LAW AND CONFLICT OF LAWS IN INTERNATIONAL COMMERCIAL ARBITRATION

by

Luca G. Radicati di Brozolo

1. As a scholar of arbitration, Emmanuel Gaillard is probably best known for his theories on the interplay between international arbitration as a system and domestic law, and on the role of what he called the "arbitral legal order", which in his vision is a body of rules from different sources that coexists with national legal systems and constitutes an important, if not the primary, source of the rules that should be applied to arbitration [1]. With this in mind, an apt way to pay tribute to him is to reflect on the rules that are applied, or should be applied, to and in international arbitration, and particularly on the respective roles in this field of domestic law (and consequently of conflict of laws) and of uniform arbitration-specific rules.

2. For the purposes of such an analysis, it is important to bear in mind that the rules governing arbitration are applied both by arbitrators and by the courts. Arbitral tribunals must apply the rules that govern whatever matter raised by the parties within the proceedings (whether relating to the merits or to any other issue) and that are therefore relevant to the exercise of their adjudicatory powers for the settlement of the dispute. The courts, for their part, must apply the rules instrumental to deciding the questions relating to arbitration that are brought before them, either in their auxiliary role with respect to arbitration (for instance the appointment or recusal of arbitrators, the validity and effects of arbitration agreements or the granting of interim measures requested of them rather than of the arbitrators) or in their supervisory role, in the context of setting aside and enforcement proceedings.

1. For this author's view on Gaillard's theory of arbitration and its contribution to the development of this institution, see L. G. Radicati di Brozolo, "Emmanuel Gaillard's Theory of International Arbitration: The Basis for a Uniform Law of International Arbitration", in *Mélanges en mémoire d'Emmanuel Gaillard*, forthcoming, 2023.

3. It is also necessary to draw a distinction between two categories of issues with respect to which rules must be applied in relation to arbitration. The first category consists of the issues relevant to the decision of the merits of the dispute.

The second category consists of the issues that pertain to the organization and functioning of arbitration as an institution or mechanism for the settlement of disputes. They include a broad variety of issues that come up every day in the practice of arbitration. These range from the ones strictly related to the conduct of the proceedings, to all the other issues that in different ways impact on the basis and the organization and functioning of the process, such as those regarding arbitrability, arbitration agreements, and in particular their validity and personal and subject-matter scope, jurisdiction, *Kompetenz-Kompetenz*, remedies, the preclusive effects of awards, *lis pendens*, the ethical obligations and conflict of interests of participants in arbitration, the sanction for the breach of the obligations of the latter, evidence (including the relative weight to be accorded to documents and witnesses), privilege, interim relief and security for costs, third party funding, the powers of arbitrators, tribunal secretaries, confidentiality, the ascertainment of the content of the law, the obligation to apply mandatory rules other than those of the chosen law, the role of arbitral precedent the methods for the calculation of damages and so on.

4. The aim of this contribution is to discuss the role that domestic law plays today in these different contexts and especially to verify whether that role is appropriate or whether instead there is room for a change of perspective and for a greater decoupling of arbitration from domestic law and, if so, how it can be achieved.

For this it is useful to begin with some thoughts on the nature and functions of arbitration, viewed from the standpoint of States and of the users – which implies considering the reasons why users have recourse to arbitration and what they expect of it – and on the relationship between arbitration and domestic legal systems. On that basis, I will then move to analyze the rules that are applied to the two types of issues identified above and the problems that their application gives rise to, in particular with a view to verifying whether the present situation complies with the expectations of users and with the defining features of international arbitration. To do this, I will consider separately the rules applied to each of the two categories of issues. I will start from the rules applied to the merits, which pose less problems, and then deal in greater detail with the rules that govern the organization and functioning of arbitration as a process, which instead raise more fundamental problems. It is in relation to the latter that Emmanuel Gaillard's thinking is particularly inspirational.

CHAPTER I

THE FUNCTION OF INTERNATIONAL ARBITRATION AND ITS RELATIONSHIP WITH DOMESTIC LEGAL SYSTEMS

5. In order to assess the suitability of the rules applied to the various aspects of arbitration it is crucial to understand the function of international arbitration and how it is viewed by the users and by States.

It is fairly uncontroversial that the participants in international commerce resort to arbitration because they feel the need for a dispute settlement mechanism better suited to their needs than domestic courts which, for the most part, they view as not being up to the task. International business seeks a mechanism that is truly international – which is to say not fragmented like the system of national courts, free from local biases, parochialisms and idiosyncrasies – and that is flexible, efficient and capable of dealing with the specificities and complexities of international transactions, greatly respectful of party autonomy and, very importantly, operates relatively predictably and uniformly across the world. International business also expects the system not to be subject to undue controls and interferences by States, although by and large it does not expect to free itself entirely from the authority of States. As a matter of fact, it actually expects the State to act as a light-handed guardian of the system, that respects the autonomy of arbitration but also ensures its proper functioning and prevents abuses.

6. This vision of the role of the State from the users' perspective is not fundamentally at odds with how States themselves nowadays perceive arbitration and with the reality of the interaction between States and arbitration.

Clearly, there is no place for the now outmoded theories elaborated in the 1960s and 1970s by the likes of Berthold Goldman, Philippe Fouchard and Clive Schmitthoff, who postulated that arbitration is the product of an autonomous legal order and can live independently, or oblivious, of national legal systems. Indeed, while arbitration is unquestionably a creature of party autonomy, it is also a creature of domestic law. It is trite that arbitration can only exist if it is accepted and supported by States and their laws, which must at a minimum enforce arbitration agreements and awards. It is worth underscoring that there is a frequent misconception as to Gaillard's position on this point. His famous representation of arbitration as based on an arbitral legal order does not amount to espousing the notion of stateless arbitration. I will come back to this, but it is important to bear in mind that Gaillard was perfectly conscious of the fundamental role of national law in the construct of arbitration [2].

7. What then is the relationship today between arbitration and the legal orders of States?

Leaving aside the somewhat sterile debate on the legal basis of arbitration, the reality is that the law of each State – both its legal system as a whole and its specific rules on arbitration – is potentially applicable to all issues relating to any given arbitration, both in front of domestic courts and in arbitral proceedings. States retain the power to exercise a very limiting and intrusive influence over arbitration, which they would certainly do were they to view it as a threat to their sovereignty or their power to apply the law and to adjudicate disputes, and more specifically if they believe it thwarts policies they consider essential. This was in fact the case until the middle of the last century when arbitration was firmly under the heel of State law. But, since the adoption of the New York Convention and the competition between legal systems it unleashed, most States which are relevant for international commerce have adopted liberal and largely convergent pro-arbitration rules and policies, which leave ample space to party autonomy and reduce to a minimum the intervention of domestic courts.

The epitome of this attitude is the broad renunciation of the review of awards at the setting aside and enforcement stages, except in exceptional and pathological situations. This is indicative, on the one hand, of a great level of trust in arbitration on the part of States and, on the other hand, of their deference to international business's desire to avoid the interference of domestic law and courts, with their innate propensity to view all problems through the lens of domestic law. A further effect of this state of things, and in particular of the broad scope of party autonomy, is the emergence of a significant body of commonly applied rules of non-State origin, of which the IBA "Rules on the Taking of Evidence in International Arbitration" are perhaps the primary example.

---

2. See E. Gaillard, *Legal Theory of International Arbitration*, Brill Nijhoff, 2010; E. Gaillard, "Theories of International Arbitration", in S. Kröll *et al.* (eds.), *Cambridge Compendium of International Commercial and Investment Arbitration*, Cambridge University Press, 2023, Vol. 1, p. 27 *et seq*. See also L. G. Radicati di Brozolo, "Emmanuel Gaillard's theory of international arbitration", *supra* note 1; D. P. Fernández Arroyo, "Emmanuel Gaillard, le positiviste", in this Volume.

8. The result is that States have allowed arbitration to flourish and to operate in relative freedom from their interference, as a transnational system of justice, albeit a decentralized and unorganized one, broadly in line with the expectations of its users. The reason for this *laissez-faire* attitude of States can only be that they consider that international arbitration is beneficial to international commerce and does not threaten the exercise of their sovereignty. And this is why they are prepared to let it flourish without unduly constricting it. Accordingly, today there is in reality fairly little conflict between arbitration and national legal systems. Of course, this is not universally the case, but it is true for the majority of States that are most relevant for international arbitration. Moreover, it is not irreversible, because even States that now have a liberal approach to arbitration could always take back control if they wished. Some recent indications of such a tendency, which it is to be hoped will remain exceptional, can be seen in the case law of some States and, even more worryingly, in that of the Court of Justice of the European Union [3].

3. See for instance the recent judgments of the French *Cour de Cassation* of 22 March 2022, *Belokon*, No. 17.17.981, *Revue de l'arbitrage*, 2022, p. 1388, and of 7 September 2022, No. 20.22.118, *Sorelec, ibid.*, p. 945, and Ch. Jarrosson, "La jurisprudence Belokon-Sorelec ou l'avènement d'un contrôle illimité des sentences", *ibid.*, p. 1267. See also German Supreme Court *(Bundesgerichtshof)*, 27 September 2022, KZB 75/21, *Vogelsberger Basaltwerk g. Constantia GmbH.* The latest decision of the Court of Justice of the European Union that is unfavorable to arbitration is the judgment of 20 June 2022, *London Steamship Owners*, C-700/20, EU:C:2022:488, commented by F. Ponzano, "The CJEU Judgment in London Steamship Owners' Mutual Insurance Association Limited v. Kingdom of Spain: A further Blow to Arbitration?", in *ICC Dispute Resolution Bulletin*, 2022, issue 3, p. 13.

On the positive side, see Belgian *Court de Cassation*, 7 April 2023, No. C.21.0325 N, *Thebelo* v. *Stölzle-Oberglass*, which overturned the non-arbitrability of disputes over exclusive distribution agreements governed by foreign law which had been a defining feature of Belgian case law for decades.

CHAPTER II

THE PRINCIPLES THAT DETERMINE THE RULES APPLICABLE IN AND TO ARBITRATION

9. With this in mind, I come to the core of the topic of this lecture, which is: what rules are applied in arbitration (by the arbitrators) and to arbitration (by the courts), how are they applied, and what is, and should be, the role of domestic law [4]?

The liberal pro-arbitration approach illustrated in the preceding chapter affects the role of domestic law both within arbitral proceedings, when the rules are applied by arbitral tribunals, and before the courts, when they are called to decide arbitration matters. Yet, there are differences between the two situations, even if there is a close relationship between the way the matter is approached in the two contexts.

10. With respect to the issues that arise within arbitral proceedings, and that are therefore to be decided by the arbitrators, States have little real interest as to whether and how their laws, both substantive and procedural, are applied, provided that their overriding mandatory rules and principles of public policy, which are aimed at protecting fundamental State interests that transcend arbitration, are respected. Indeed, in keeping with the principle of party autonomy, domestic laws never prescribe their own application, or that of any other domestic law (even by default) to any issue that arises within arbitration, unless the parties agree thereto in respect of given matters. Actually, domestic arbitration laws, as well as arbitration rules, contain practically no precepts, and certainly no binding ones, specifically regarding the rules to be applied in arbitration and thus leave the parties (and, failing agreement between them, the arbitrators) the broadest freedom to determine the norms to be applied. In fact, the only mandatory rule on the norms to be applied in arbitration is the one requiring the respect

4. These themes are also treated in other recent works of this author: see L. G. Radicati di Brozolo, "Domestic Law and Conflict of Laws: What should their Role be in International Arbitration?", in G. Cordero Moss and D. P. Fernández Arroyo, *Applicable Law Issues in International Arbitration*, forthcoming, 2023; L. G. Radicati di Brozolo, "What Rules must Arbitrators apply to Decide according to the Law", in *Arbitration international*, 2023, forthcoming; D. P. Fernández Arroyo and L. G. Radicati di Brozolo, "The Proper Role of the Seat in International Commercial Arbitration: A Minimalist Perspective", in *Essays in Honor of Piero Bernardini*, forthcoming.

of due process and the right to be heard. Significantly, when this rule is contained in arbitration rules it does not even refer to any specific domestic principles.

11. In light of this, it may be surprising that domestic law continues to play a major role within international arbitration, both with respect to decisions on the merits and with respect to those on issues relating to the functioning of arbitration. As discussed below, this is due in large part to a totally misplaced belief of many arbitrators that domestic law is the obligatory, or at least the primary, go-to framework for the solution of the problems that arise in connection with arbitration. It is also due to the fact that applying domestic law gives a (false) sense of security, as if doing so would render arbitrators less liable to criticism than if they applied more well-considered and appropriate solutions.

In turn, this is based on a lack of understanding of the level of freedom that States grant to arbitration and of what should be the correct approach to the governance of the latter in keeping with its nature and functions as a dispute settlement mechanism distinct from domestic litigation. Too often arbitrators are unduly preoccupied that the disregard of national law, particularly the one of the seat, may entail the set aside of their award. However, this concern is only justified insofar as it is assumed that the courts too will fail to appreciate that the majority of the rules of the law of their jurisdiction which might be considered applicable to arbitration are actually not necessarily applicable to it, and in any case are not of such crucial importance as to form part of public policy, which would be the sole ground for the annulment of the award.

12. The assumption that courts will be prone to annul awards for breaching, or not applying, rules of domestic law, is overstated. It is true that, when issues relating to arbitration arise before them, courts tend to apply domestic law, most frequently their own. Nonetheless, in keeping with their restrictive pro-arbitration interpretation of public policy, when they exercise their supervisory function in setting aside proceedings, they increasingly accept that the disregard of domestic rules and principles, even important ones, does not entail a breach of public policy justifying the annulment of the award. This is particularly the case when the decisions of arbitrators are in line with established practices or rules developed within the arbitral system. This is for example what happens with respect to rules on the conduct of the arbitral proceedings, with regard to which courts recognize that the

applicable rules are not those of domestic procedural law but those routinely applied in international arbitral practice.

13. In the following Chapters I will endeavor to show in more detail how the different types of issues are decided in international arbitration and to explain why the current role played by domestic law is unjustified and excessive, what the deficiencies of this situation are and what in my view is the correct approach to achieve a greater enfranchisement of international arbitration from domestic law (and conflicts of law). To do so I will first address the rules relating to the decision of the merits of the dispute, which pose fewer difficulties and drawbacks, and then turn to those relating to the functioning of arbitration as a system for conflict resolution.

CHAPTER III

THE RULES FOR THE RESOLUTION OF THE MERITS OF THE DISPUTE

A. The predominance of domestic law

14. The question of the rules applicable to the merits in international arbitration arises almost exclusively before arbitral tribunals. In fact, when disputes are devolved to arbitration the potential involvement of domestic courts in respect of the merits only occurs at the setting aside or enforcement stage [5], in the event that the compatibility of the awards with substantive public policy is contested. Save if they find serious violations of truly fundamental principles, in that context national courts tend to show little interest in their law being applied correctly or even being applied at all.

15. Within arbitration, the application of domestic rules to the resolution of the merits is widespread and almost universal. This is fairly understandable and not *per se* problematic. The rules applicable to the decision of the merits are the subject of one of the only two rules that deal with the rules to be applied in arbitration (the other one being the one on the rules on the conduct of the proceedings that will be discussed below). This rule, which is present in practically all arbitration laws and rules [6], is modeled on the traditional conflict rule on the law governing contracts. In its original form, it provided that the arbitrators apply the law (meaning a domestic law) chosen by the parties or, failing a choice, the law determined by the arbitrators according to a conflict of laws methodology that varied slightly from one rule to the other. The rule has now evolved and in most cases allows the parties to choose non-national rules instead of a domestic law and the arbitrators to apply those rules even in the absence of a specific designation by the parties. At the same time, arbitrators are no longer held to apply a strict conflict

5. Provisions such as Section 69 of the English Arbitration Act 1996 and Article 829, para. 3 of Italian Code of Civil Procedure, Article, which permit appeals against awards on points of law are by now exceptional and generally opted out of by the parties.

6. See for instance Article 17 *et seq.* of the UNCITRAL Model Law on International Arbitration; Section 38 of the English Arbitration Act 1996; Article 182 of the Swiss Private International Law Statute; Article 28 of the ICC Rules; Article 25 of the LCIA Rules.

of laws approach to establish the applicable law in the absence of a designation by the parties [7].

16. Despite the freedom not to designate a domestic law and to opt instead for non-national rules, and the wealth of rules from a variety of non-national sources that could provide excellent alternatives to domestic law for many cross-border disputes, the parties still almost invariably designate a domestic law as the governing law. Save in exceptional circumstances, in the presence of a choice of a domestic law the arbitrators must abide by it, lest they incur in a failure to respect the instructions of the parties, potentially entailing a set aside of the award. Even in the absence of a choice of the applicable rules by the parties, the application of State law remains the preferred solution of arbitrators, although they are not required to do so, as illustrated above.

The fact that the parties predominantly choose domestic law in lieu of non-national rules to govern the merits of their dispute, and that arbitrators too tend to apply domestic law even where they are not bound to do so by a designation of such a law by the parties, can in my view largely be explained by the innate conservatism of contract drafters, as well as of counsel and arbitrators, who are loath to leave the beaten path when it comes to choosing the rules governing contracts, and are still unaware of the potential advantages of non-State rules in certain circumstances.

B. How domestic law is applied to the merits in arbitration

17. As I have discussed elsewhere [8], even where the applicable rules are those of domestic law, there may in practice be differences between how those rules are applied in arbitration and before domestic courts. The differences may be greater or lesser depending on a variety of factors. To name just a few, the nature of the transaction, of the dispute and of the business sectors involved and whether they are typical of cross-border commerce or more similar to purely domestic ones and whether there exist specific international practices and contractual models for the type of transaction in question, as well as the nationality and characteristics of the parties (including their experience and sophistication).

---

7. See L. G. Radicati di Brozolo, "Party Autonomy and the Rules governing the Merits of the Dispute in Commercial Arbitration", in F. Ferrari (ed.), *Limits to Party Autonomy in International Commercial Arbitration*, Juris, 2016, pp. 331-362.

8. L. G. Radicati di Brozolo, "Party Autonomy", *supra* note 7, p. 352 *et seq*.

The preference of international business for arbitration over domestic court litigation is a powerful indication that it seeks to eschew the parochialism of the latter in favor of arbitration's more transnational and business-oriented and less formalistic approach, which is better suited to deal with the peculiarities and complexities of international transactions and may warrant a different treatment than purely domestic ones. All these factors inform the parties' expectations as to the functioning of the arbitral process, including potentially as to how the relevant rules will be applied. Depending on the situation, there may be a more or less implied assumption that the choice of an arbitral forum implies an application of the applicable rules, even of those of domestic law, more in line with business and international practices, and therefore less punctilious than would be the case before a court of the relevant jurisdiction.

18. The difference in the way the rules are applied in international arbitration compared to domestic litigation also has to do with the legal and professional background of the arbitrators. Arbitrators often are more knowledgeable than judges of the specificities of international transactions and of the business sector involved and are chosen for that reason more than for the specific knowledge of the applicable law, so much so that arbitrators are frequently not qualified in the applicable law (as not infrequently occurs for counsel in arbitration). Moreover, unlike domestic judges, arbitrators are not organs of a State and are therefore concerned only about the dispute before them, and not about ensuring the consistency of the legal system and the furtherance of its policies. All this explains why many times arbitrators are the ones who elaborate modern and business-appropriate solutions that then trickle down into domestic law (to mention one example the rules on hardship in long-term contracts). Arbitrators also have a greater leeway than domestic courts to rely on arbitral precedents, which can provide important inspiration for their decisions [9]. Obviously, in applying the applicable rules, especially if they depart from established solutions, arbitrators must be particularly attentive to the explicit or presumable intentions of the parties.

19. A specific example of the difference between how the law may be treated in arbitration and before domestic courts has to do with the scope of party autonomy. As I have advocated previously [10], the complete

9. L. G. Radicati di Brozolo, "La valeur du précédent en arbitrage commercial international", *Revue de l'arbitrage*, 2023, p. 37 *et seq*.

10. L. G. Radicati di Brozolo, "Party Autonomy", *supra* note 7, p. 354 *et seq*.

freedom of the parties to choose the rules governing their transaction also has the consequence that they are permitted to displace the "simple" mandatory rules of the applicable law, even the one designated by them. This is typically the case where the contract contains detailed and heavily negotiated provisions on a certain issue, which may not be in line with the provisions (including the mandatory ones) of the applicable law. This is clearly something that would not be permissible before domestic courts, but is perfectly compatible with the autonomy of the parties in arbitration. The premise is obviously that there exists an agreement of the parties to so derogate from the mandatory provisions. The second premise is that this is permissible only in respect of simple mandatory rules (those that can be derogated from by the choice of another law) and not of "overriding mandatory rules", which can never be derogated from, regardless of the applicable law [11]. This situation typically arises in relation to the many types of contracts routinely used across the world that are based on similar models that govern the relationship in minute detail and are often heavily negotiated with the involvement of experienced professionals and little or no regard for the applicable law (which is often determined as an afterthought). Notorious examples are contracts for mergers and acquisitions and construction. With respect to such contracts, it is incongruous to allow ex post dissatisfied parties to extricate themselves from the agreed contractual language and standardized practices by leveraging on general rules that do not fit well with the agreed contractual regime and presumably not envisaged during the negotiations.

C. Conclusions on the role of domestic law with respect to the merits

20. The predominance of domestic law for the decision of the merits in international arbitration is not problematic and not in contrast with the nature and functions of this dispute resolution mechanism, although it may appear somewhat incongruous and perhaps excessive because it does not take full advantage of the potential of arbitration. As mentioned, the developing body of relatively detailed and sophisticated

11. The reference here is to "simple" mandatory rules, i.e. those that cannot be derogated from by party autonomy when the law to which they belong is the governing law. These differ from "overriding mandatory rules" mentioned above, which remain applicable even when the governing law is a different one (see Art. 9 of the (Rome I) Regulation 593/2008 on the law applicable to contractual obligations).

non-national rules (foremost amongst which the Unidroit principles of international commercial contracts) can in many cases provide a viable alternative to domestic laws and may be applied more broadly as those rules become better known and understood.

21. That said, domestic law is perfectly suited to the solution of most substantive issues brought to arbitration, especially since in arbitration it can be applied with greater flexibility than before domestic courts to take into consideration the specificities of cross-border transactions. Most importantly, its application corresponds to the intent of the parties, who in fact designate it to govern their transaction in the majority of cases. And of course, given that the merits by definition have to be decided on a case-by-case basis, there is not the same need for uniform solutions which instead exists for the issues relating to the functioning of arbitration as a process. There is consequently no need to develop arbitration-specific rules for the merits, even though some degree of uniformity in the solutions may be appropriate. This can in part be achieved by a broader reliance on arbitral case law, which is however stymied by the confidentiality of awards.

22. Finally, with regard to the merits the identification of the applicable rules is relatively straightforward, especially since those are usually specifically designated by the parties, and even when they are not the approaches are relatively well-trodden. There is a debate as to whether the parties are also permitted to designate the rules on matters other than those governed by the *lex causae*, which in my view should be resolved in favor of party autonomy, but this issue arises relatively infrequently and does not pose major practical problems. Thus, the recourse to conflict of laws with respect to issues of merits does not have the same nefarious effects it has with regard to the issues relating to the arbitral process.

CHAPTER IV

THE RULES RELATING TO THE ARBITRAL PROCESS

23. As mentioned, domestic law also plays a significant role in respect of many issues other than the merits, i.e. those that relate to the basis and functioning of arbitration as a dispute settlement process. However, unlike for the merits, the application of domestic law in this context is much less justified and more problematic and, as I will show, is compatible neither with the spirit of international arbitration nor with the expectations of the users, for whom it is aimed to constitute a truly transnational system of justice.

A distinction has to be made in this connection between, on the one hand, the issues relating strictly to the conduct of the proceedings and, on the other hand, all the other issues that may arise in relation to an arbitration [12].

A. The rules on the conduct of the proceedings

24. The rules on the conduct of the proceedings, or procedural rules as they are sometimes called, are those that govern the practical functioning of an arbitration. They are the ones that regulate how the parties plead their case, the sequence of written and oral pleadings, the hearing, the taking and assessment of evidence and similar matters. Like the ones on the merits, these rules too are applied exclusively by arbitral tribunals, and the role of the courts is simply to assess that in applying them arbitrators do not incur in violations of due process.

25. This type of rule is the subject of the second of the only two rules normally contained in arbitration laws and arbitration rules that determine the rules to be applied by the arbitrators, which can be termed arbitration-specific conflict norms (the other one being the one on the rules governing the merits discussed above). As is well known, that rule provides that the rules on the conduct of the proceedings are

---

12. See para. 3 above. These issues have been termed "twilight issues" by G. A. Bermann, who addresses them comprehensively in his recent book *Twilight Issues in International Arbitration: Latent Choice of Law Issues*, Kluwer, 2023.

agreed by the parties and, failing such agreement, are determined by the arbitrators [13].

26. As previously noted, it is now routinely accepted that the rules of civil procedure that apply before domestic courts (including specifically those of the law of the seat) are not applicable (at least mandatorily) in arbitration, and that their disregard does not entail a breach of public policy. Such rules therefore do not interfere with the freedom of the parties and arbitral tribunals to select the rules governing their proceedings.

In practice the parties seldom if ever directly lay down the rules on the conduct of the proceedings, although they often do so by adhering to arbitration rules, particularly those of an arbitral institution. But even these rules do not govern the issues in detail.

27. Because of the almost universal recognition, at least by arbitration experts, that there is no room for domestic procedural law in international arbitration, the conduct of the proceedings is the only area of arbitration with respect to which nowadays domestic law and conflict of laws play almost no role. There now exists a fairly well-developed body of rules and practices that are applied consistently in international arbitrations and which have been developed also thanks to institutions like the Arbitration Committee of the International Bar Association. As a result of this evolution, the users of arbitration can count on a core of international arbitration procedure, which contributes to the uniformity and predictability of the conduct of the proceedings, in line with the spirit of arbitration and permits it to be considered a transnational system of justice.

The inapplicability of domestic law to purely procedural issues within arbitration is also ratified by domestic courts, as noted in paragraph 12 above.

B. The inadequacy of domestic law to govern matters relating to the arbitral process

28. The situation is apparently more complex when it comes to issues relating to the arbitral process other than those governing the

---

13. See for instance Article 182 of the Swiss Private International Law Act (which still contains an outdated provision according to which may determine the arbitral procedure, including by submitting to "the procedural law of their choice"); Article 19 of the UNCITRAL Model Law; Article 1509 of the French Code of Civil Procedure; Article 17.1 of the UNCITRAL Arbitration Rules; Article 19 of the ICC Rules ("Rules governing the proceedings"); Article 14 of the LCIA Rules.

simple conduct of the proceedings. For these issues, of which there are a myriad [14] and which arise with considerable frequency, primarily before arbitrators but also come before courts at the stage of the review of the award, there is no equivalent of the two arbitration-specific conflict rules relating respectively to the merits and to the conduct of the proceedings. Yet, the principle that arbitrators have no obligation to apply domestic law applies here too. Notwithstanding this, when it comes to this type of question, and unlike for the conduct of the proceedings, arbitrators still tend to resort to domestic law, for the untenable reasons outlined in Chapter 2 above.

29. The application of domestic law to the issues at hand poses a range of problems. The first one is a conflict of laws issue that arises due to the need to identify which, amongst the domestic laws amongst the many with which an international arbitration by definition has contacts, is to be applied. Differently to issues of merits, in respect of these issues the parties are unlikely to have designated the applicable rules. Of course, if they had, the designation would also have to be respected in these cases.

On this point, the approach is marginally different, depending on whether the issue arises before a national court or an arbitral tribunal. National courts at least do not have to worry about which set of conflict rules to turn to for this exercise, since they must apply their own legal system. Arbitrators, on the other hand, lack a conflict of laws system of their own and, unless they opt for the *voie directe*, must determine which conflict system or approach to follow, both of which leave them with a broad margin of discretion. This means that the solution to the conflict of laws, and therefore the identification of the rules that will be applied, will vary from one case to the other, not necessarily rationally or predictably, with a high likelihood that the law applicable to the same issue or type of issue will differ depending on where the issue arises (and the preferences of the adjudicator). This is not in line with the objective of arbitration which strives – or should strive – to be a uniform system, which presupposes the application of the same rules to deal with a given category of issue.

30. The second problem is that, even when a supposedly suitable conflict of laws system or approach has been identified, for many matters having to do with the functioning of arbitration, the specific conflict rule for the issue at hand may be difficult to identify with precision.

---

14. See para. 3 above.

What is the law applicable to the validity and effects of an arbitration agreement? or to the granting of an interim measure, or confidentiality? There are different approaches to these questions and the solution may not be straightforward even within a given legal system. The result is an additional margin of discretion on the part of the adjudicator and ultimately a great uncertainty as to the legal system within which the relevant rules to govern the issue will have to be sought. The uncertainty and discretion are not mitigated by the approach based on the characterization of the issue as pertaining to procedure or to the merits, often held to entail the application respectively the law of the seat or that of the merits. This is because the characterization of many issues as pertaining to procedure or the merits may be difficult if not impossible, and in any case is not consistent from one legal system to the other.

31. The third problem is that the national law eventually considered applicable will often not contain specific rules for all the issues that arise in arbitration. The consequence may be the application of rules of that law that apply to similar problems in domestic litigation, but may well not be suitable to arbitration. A good example are the rules on *res judicata*, which exist in each legal system. These rules not only vary from one legal system to the other, but even more significantly refer to the *res judicata* effect of domestic judgments and in no way take into consideration the specificities of international arbitration and awards. Relying on such rules may yield results that vary significantly depending on the conflict-of-laws approach adopted by the adjudicator and may be unsatisfactory in the context of arbitration. The same may be true of many other issues, for example ethics, in respect of which the application of domestic law on the basis of conflict of laws leads to unworkable solutions [15].

32. This inaptitude of national law to govern arbitration also applies to the law of the seat, which is often considered to govern a broad range of issues and to constitute the starting point for the solution of arbitration-related issues. In reality, the seat is not a particularly significant connecting factor for a variety of reasons. I will just say that this is so even when it is designated by the parties, including sophisticated ones, because generally their focus is on the reputation of its courts and their experience in dealing with arbitrations in an efficient, unbiased, non-

15. L. G. Radicati di Brozolo and F. Ponzano, "The Need for Arbitration-Specific Rules on Ethics: A Plea for a Collective Effort", in *Leadership, Legitimacy, Legacy: A Tribute to Alexis Mourre*, CCI, 2023, pp. 105 *et seq.*

parochial and pro-arbitration manner, in line with the prevailing trends in international arbitration. However, it is extremely unlikely that, when choosing the seat, parties will give particular thought to how its law deals with the countless issues likely to arise in an arbitration or would expect that the rules of that law will be applicable to their arbitration. For example, the interpretation and effects of the arbitration agreement, including its binding force on non-signatories, the *res judicata* effect of the award, the conditions for granting interim measures or allowing third-party funding. In many cases the rules governing those issues (in particular those applicable to arbitration) may not even be readily recognizable beforehand, because they will not be spelled out in formal rules and there may often not be any pertinent or unequivocal case law. So, recourse to the law of the seat – which moreover often lacks meaningful contacts with the dispute – does not significantly improve predictability and has the same drawbacks as any other domestic law. The only reason for taking it into consideration is to ensure that the award will not fall foul of its principles of public policy, which however as illustrated above is increasingly less likely to be the case [16].

33. To summarize, applying domestic law to the issues that arise in connection with arbitration leads to unsatisfactory results. This is because of the uncertainty and subjectiveness inherent in the identification of the applicable law, due to the lack of clear conflict rules; the fact that domestic legal systems will often not contain clear rules on the issues at stake, with the consequence that rules governing similar issues before domestic courts will be applied by analogy or extension, without a proper verification of their suitability to arbitration; and the fact that the relevant rules in any case are likely to vary from one domestic system to another. This is detrimental to predictability and to the uniformity of solutions, as these vary depending on which law is applied, and entails the application of rules not specifically tailored to arbitration, all of which is at odds with the spirit and goals of arbitration and the expectations of the users that arbitration operate as a true system of transnational justice.

16. For the view that the importance of the law of the seat tends to be overestimated see also G. A. Bermann, *Twilight Issues*, *supra* note 12, p. 50.

CHAPTER V

WHAT RULES FOR THE OTHER MATTERS RELATING TO THE ARBITRAL PROCESS?

34. The foregoing conclusion that relying on domestic law for arbitration-related matters is unnecessary and, more importantly, inconsistent with the spirit and nature of international arbitration raises the question of which rules to apply to those matters in keeping with that spirit, without an indiscriminate and unprincipled recourse to domestic law.

A. Within arbitration

35. When the issues arise before arbitrators, the starting point must obviously be the agreement of the parties, or possibly their expectations insofar as they can be discerned in light of the context. Absent cogent indications to the contrary, there is no reason to assume that the parties envisage that domestic law should govern questions other than the merits.

When there is no agreement or the expectations are not evident, which will most often be the case, it is for arbitral tribunals to find the appropriate solution, which may vary depending on whether or not they can rely on a suitable transnational approach to the question at hand.

(a) *The recourse to accepted transnational solutions*

36. As a first step, arbitrators should attempt to identify any sufficiently consolidated arbitration-specific solutions or tendencies. This would be relatively easy to the extent that there exist rules or soft law instruments or commonly accepted practices specifically relevant to the question before them. This type of rule, however, for the moment exists primarily for the conduct of the proceedings (in particular the IBA "Rules on the taking of Evidence in International Arbitration" recalled above). The IBA "Guidelines on Conflict of Interests in International Arbitration" are an example of such rules for other types of issues, but the problem they govern rarely if ever has to be decided by arbitrators.

37. For certain questions there are however converging, or at least prevailing, trends that can form the basis for a transnational solution. Interim measures and security for costs are a good example. By now there is a body of arbitral case-law, as well as of rules in arbitration rules [17], dealing specifically with these topics without reference to domestic law that provides an important source of inspiration for arbitral tribunals confronted with them. Inspiration can come not only from commercial precedents, but also from the jurisprudence of international courts and investor-State tribunals, given that they are in a position similar to international commercial tribunals insofar as they lack hard and fast rules on this kind of matter and operate on the basis of a consensual process governed by party autonomy and to which domestic law is not necessarily applicable [18].

In situations such as these, there is no justification for applying domestic law, and in fact arbitrators increasingly take into consideration and adopt transnational solutions. As a matter of fact, the amenability of arbitrators to resort to such solutions rather than to domestic law when they are able to rely on existing transnational practices and arbitral precedents is a clear sign that there is no requirement to apply domestic law and that doing so is only a conditional reflex not dictated by any well-considered reasoning. The now unanimously accepted recourse to a transnational body of rules on the conduct of the proceedings is therefore the model to be followed whenever transnational solutions have developed.

38. But transnational solutions can also be sought for issues in respect of which there is no broadly accepted arbitral practice, such as those just recalled. This is where Emmanuel Gaillard's teaching becomes particularly pertinent. Gaillard has shown that on many – but of course not all – problems relating to arbitration there exists today a non-negligible degree of similarity in the solutions of arbitral case law as well as of the jurisprudence on arbitration of many States. This incipient body of transnational solutions is the essence of what Gaillard has famously called the arbitral legal order, which is the core of an emerging uniform law of arbitration and which, it is again

17. See for instance ICC Rules, Article 28; UNCITRAL Rules, Article 17; UNCITRAL Model Law, Article 17 *et seq*. For an analysis of the rules governing the granting of interim measures in arbitration, see J. Fouret and Ch. Seraglini, "Provisional Measures by Arbitrators and Emergency Arbitration", in *Cambridge Compendium*, *supra* note 2, p. 1211 *et seq*, showing that domestic rules play a residual role.

18. See L.G. Radicati di Brozolo, "La valeur du précédent en arbitrage commercial international", *supra* note 9.

worth underscoring, is not antagonistic to domestic legal orders, the role of which is very present in his thinking [19]. Gaillard theorized that it is essential to concentrate not on the differences, but rather on the commonalities between the approaches to arbitration issues in the various domestic legal systems. These can be exploited to find suitable solutions. It bears keeping in mind that where there are divergences between domestic approaches, often they are not due to profound reasons of principle or to the need to safeguard different fundamental interests. The specific solutions to arbitration problems of individual domestic systems are often a reflection of tradition and of a passive adherence to, or an extrapolation of, solutions prevailing in the legal system in question. These are followed without consideration of the broader context beyond the four corners of that system capable of establishing whether different solutions, more in tune with the particularities of arbitration or with solutions of other legal systems, might not be equally compatible with the system.

39. This means that domestic law need not always be disregarded *a priori* by arbitrators and can even provide a starting point for their decisions. However, the focus should not be on individual domestic laws, however identified, but rather on whatever common principles and approaches may be gleaned from them. The attitude when considering domestic law to address the problems of international arbitration should be similar to the one required in the application of uniform law. This means, not in an inward looking, parochial, way but with a view to ensuring consistency within the system of arbitration.

Thus, where transnational approaches can be found – even if they have not acquired a more formal status, such as that of rules incorporated in instruments of soft law (such as the IBA "Rules on the Taking of Evidence in International Arbitration") – arbitrators should take inspiration from them and use them as a basis for their decisions, in a transnational mindset.

19. See E. Gaillard, "Legal Theory of International Arbitration", Brill Nijhoff, 2010; E. Gaillard, "Theories of International Arbitration", in S. Kröll *et al.* (eds.), *Cambridge Compendium of International Commercial and Investment Arbitration*, Cambridge University Press, 2023, 27. On Gaillard's theory, see L. G. Radicati di Brozolo, "Emmanuel Gaillard's Theory of International Arbitration: The Basis for a Uniform Law of International Arbitration", *supra* note 1; D. P. Fernández Arroyo, "Emmanuel Gaillard, le positiviste", *supra*, note 2.

(b) *The need to identify ad hoc solutions in the absence of transnational ones*

The situation is admittedly less simple when arbitrators cannot ground their decisions on sufficiently established transnational solutions or on a relative uniformity or convergence between domestic laws. Nevertheless, not even in these situations is there any justification for not attempting to elaborate arbitration-specific solutions and to fall back on a specific domestic law. Arbitrators must always be conscious of their inherent or implied powers to deal with situations not caught by the parties' agreement or by relevant rules specifically designed for arbitration. These powers provide the basis for seeking the appropriate solution for the case at hand [20]. Of course, they ought to be exercised with due care, in light of all the relevant circumstances, but always being mindful of the specificities of international arbitration and the fact that it is a system in its own right, which must be governed by practices and rules designed to reflect its peculiarities and not necessarily mirroring the idiosyncrasies of individual domestic legal systems.

40. It is noteworthy that the goal of identifying the proper solution for an arbitration-related problem in a given case is not to arrive at a solution shared by all legal systems, or even just by those to which the arbitration has a connection, which could be impossible if the laws in question are not very similar or lead to outcomes not responsive to the needs of arbitration. Rather, the goal is to find solutions specifically suited to those needs. It should therefore not be a problem that the solution ultimately adopted by the arbitrators may be more similar to those of certain legal domestic systems than to those of others, since the only objective is its responsiveness to the needs of arbitration. After all, that is the approach that prevails for the conduct of the proceedings and evidence, the rules on which have developed according to a model more in line with those of common law systems than with others, largely because they have been found to be better suited to the needs of arbitration.

41. There is no serious ground for the objection, often raised, that the search by arbitrators for appropriate *ad hoc* solutions tailored to

20. International Law Association, *ILA Report on the Inherent Powers of Arbitrators in International Commercial Arbitration*, Report for the Biennial Conference in Washington DC, 2014; L. G. Radicati di Brozolo, "Applying the Rules governing the Merits in International Commercial Arbitration – What Role for inherent Powers", in F. Ferrari (ed.), *Inherent Powers in International Adjudication*, Juris, 2018, p. 269 *et seq.*, especially 291 *et seq.*

arbitration is conducive to uncertainty. Of course, this does leave a certain amount of discretion to the arbitrators. However, that discretion is no greater than the one highlighted above, which is intrinsic to the pure and simple application of domestic law by way of conflict of laws, and additionally leads to lack of uniformity and to solutions that do not even make a pretense of responding to the needs of arbitration. It is sufficient to consider that the choice that arbitrators seeking to apply domestic law have to make between, say, the rules of the law of the seat or those on the law governing the merits, or any other law, is totally arbitrary, since none of those laws has any greater objective specific title to be applied to the issues relating to the arbitral process than other ones. Arbitrators therefore cannot be faulted for arbitrariness if they decide on the strength of a focused arbitration specific approach rather than by applying domestic law.

42. Furthermore, the course advocated here should not create a risk of the solutions reached by the arbitrators being held to conflict with public policy if they are contested before domestic judges. If the nature of public policy is properly understood, and if it is understood that arbitration need not operate according to the principles of domestic law, the courts should have no reason to quibble with arbitral solutions not aligned to established solutions in domestic law. This, as already emphasized, is what already occurs for the rules on the conduct of the proceedings [21]. Needless to say, the more the decisions of arbitrators are perceived as being in line with other arbitral precedents or arbitral practice, even if not sufficiently well-established, the greater will the willingness of courts be to view the departure of arbitrators from domestic solutions according to a parochial lens.

43. Therefore, arbitrators should not be shy to exercise their powers in order to find the appropriate solution for the case at hand. After all, important transnational rules – such as the ones on *Kompetenz-Kompetenz* and arbitral interim measures – have emerged from the willingness of arbitral tribunals to do so without passively adhering to domestic law.

In conclusion, the approach to all arbitration-related issues, except for the merits, should be the same one that is codified in the universal rule valid for the conduct of the proceedings, according to which, absent an agreement of the parties, the applicable rules are determined by the arbitrators. This of course leaves room for the application of any

21. See above, para. 12.

relevant transnational rules or practices, which should actually be the preferred solution. Domestic law should therefore be applicable only to the merits, in the way illustrated in Chapter III above.

B. Before the courts

44. When the matters in question are to be decided directly by courts, as mentioned these will almost invariably apply domestic law. That said, despite that the obligatory starting point for them is the *lex fori* (including its conflict rules), it is not inconceivable that, with the emergence of transnational rules or practices, or at least approaches common to more than one legal system, courts may be prepared to adhere to a less parochial outlook. This implies acknowledging that domestic rules and principles may either not be applied at all if they are unsuitable to the specificities of international arbitration, or may be applied in a way that is more in line with these. This possibility is demonstrated by the acceptance by national courts of well-established transnational rules such as those elaborated by the IBA, which trump their domestic rules of procedure [22].

45. Where transnational solutions, beyond those strictly relating to the conduct of arbitral proceedings, can be identified, courts – like arbitrators – should take them into consideration in deciding questions connected to arbitration. Courts are not outright precluded from doing so. Indeed, the domestic rules they might consider relevant – be they the ones specific to arbitration contained in the arbitration law or other rules they might consider applying to arbitration by analogy or extension – are for the most part not mandatory, so that they can be adapted or derogated from if appropriate. Accordingly, in many instances this should allow national judges to abandon parochial conceptions standing in the way of the consistency with the system of international arbitration, unless they are demonstratively driven by serious policy concerns relevant to arbitration.

46. The spirit should be similar to the one governing the application of uniform law [23]. Although, technically speaking, arbitration law as a whole is not uniform law, the two rules of the New York Convention – the obligations to give effect to arbitration agreements and to recognize and enforce arbitral awards – are uniform law binding on all contracting

---

22. See para. 27 above.
23. L. G. Radicati di Brozolo, "Emmanuel Gaillard's Theory of International Arbitration", *supra* note 1.

States that set forth the pivotal principles of the system of international arbitration. And as a matter of fact, as highlighted by the UNCITRAL Guide to the New York Convention co-edited by Emmanuel Gaillard, the Convention's harmonizing spirit has been faithfully respected by the Contracting States, which "have interpreted and applied the New York Convention in an overwhelmingly consistent manner and [their] courts have diverged from the trends in the case law in only isolated instances" [24].

The influence of the New York Convention, which has been defined a "constitutional instrument" [25], can go, and indeed has gone, beyond the letter of the two rules it lays down. If properly understood and applied, those rules – in particular the obligation to give effect to arbitration agreements – exert a powerful influence on the entire spectrum of arbitration law, because, as rules of uniform law, they mandate a pro-arbitration interpretation and application of many rules of national law in order to ensure the Convention's *effet utile* [26]. The Convention thus provides a powerful tool for domestic judges to interpret and apply their domestic law in a way that ensures its consistency with the spirit and objectives of arbitration.

24. The UNCITRAL Secretariat Guide on the New York Convention, E. Gaillard and G. A. Bermann (eds.), Brill Nijhoff, 2017, xv.

25. Gary Born, International Commercial Arbitration 117, Wolters Kluwer, 3rd ed., 2021.

26. *Id.* at 104 *et seq.*

CHAPTER VI

THE NEED TO ELABORATE TRANSNATIONAL NORMS FOR ARBITRATION-RELATED MATTERS

47. The proposition that, in the absence of accepted transnational solution to turn to, arbitrators must elaborate *ad hoc* solutions, refraining from resorting to domestic law as a matter of course, is consistent with the principle that domestic law is not the appropriate source to govern arbitration-related matters. Although it arguably leads to better results than the application of domestic law, this course of action is far from ideal. It is inefficient because it is a source of uncertainty and procedural incidents, with the attendant costs and waste of time and the prospect of divergent outcomes detrimental to uniformity, and it imposes a burden and an added responsibility on arbitral tribunals.

In the long run, arbitral practice and case law permits the emergence of common solutions, as occurred for interim measures [27], but this can be a long process, especially given the still limited availability of commercial arbitral jurisprudence.

48. The solution can therefore only be the elaboration of specific rules to tackle these problems. Clearly, such rules cannot come from States, whether by domestic law or international conventions. For one thing, this would be a lengthy process and would be at odds with the non-interventionist attitude of States towards arbitration and would introduce rigidities and produce potentially divergent solutions. The solution could not even come from a harmonization of conflict rules, as these would not eliminate the lack of overall uniformity that would derive from the divergences in the solutions dictated by different substantive domestic laws.

The only alternative are soft law instruments, such as those developed by the IBA and the International Law Association [28], which have done a highly commendable job of elaborating, and in some cases updating, important rules, guidelines and recommendations. The success of these

---

27. See para. 37 above.

28. See the Reports and Recommendations of the ILA International Arbitration Committee on "Public Policy as a Bar to the Enforcement of International Arbitral Awards" (2002), "*Lis Pendens* and *Res Judicata* in International Arbitration" (2006), "Ascertaining the Contents of the Applicable Law in International Commercial Arbitration" (2008), "Confidentiality in International Commercial Arbitration" (2010).

instruments has been unequal, and perhaps none have achieved the level of acceptance as the IBA's "Rules on the Taking of Evidence in International Arbitration" and "Guidelines on Conflicts of Interest in International Arbitration".

49. Strangely, these efforts are also subject to criticism, including because they supposedly introduce rigidities in arbitration by reducing flexibility for the parties and constrain the freedom of arbitrators (some even speak of their artistic creativity) and impose a one size fits all. A purported lack "democratic legitimacy" is also at times evoked, as is the fact that the solutions adopted by the soft law instruments are not common to all systems, and especially that they tend to adopt common law models. This criticism was for example initially levelled at the IBA Rules on Evidence which are now universally accepted, and for example is still mentioned in connection with the ILA Recommendations on *res judicata*.

With the utmost respect, I suggest that such criticism is unprincipled. It is manifestly not true that this type of rule stifles creativity and party autonomy. Soft law rules are by definition not mandatory and allow parties and arbitrators to devise their own solutions if they prefer. But they provide a useful starting point, that avoids reinventing the wheel with each new arbitration and, importantly, they reduce the discretion of arbitral tribunals and the unpredictability of the solutions they are obliged to invent in the absence of rules. The same is true of the lack of legitimacy and the fact that the rules may be more closely aligned to the approaches of certain legal cultures than others. Actually, the greater the divergences between the different domestic laws, the greater is the need to devise uniform solutions. Once the rules are developed, they are available to parties and arbitrators, but can be disregarded where they are felt not to reflect the desired approach in any given case. However, as already explained [29], there is no reason to forsake a solution that is considered in keeping with the needs of arbitration simply because it is not common to all legal systems and cultures.

50. The IBA Rules on Evidence are a case in point. Initially they were criticized, in large part because they reflected common law approaches (which is true only in part, because they are a much watered down version of US rules on evidence). However, they have gradually gained acceptance and are now very broadly applied or used as a baseline for decisions in arbitral proceedings, simply because they are considered

29. See para. 41 above.

useful and well-suited to arbitration. Predictably, some continue to criticize them, now on the grounds that the solutions they provide are not efficient [30], and it may well be that changes or alternatives will be proposed. There have indeed been concrete attempts to find alternatives, like the Prague Rules, although they have not gained much traction, which however shows the flexibility of the system. In the meantime, until different rules are elaborated or the current ones are revised if the need for that is sufficiently broadly recognized, the IBA Rules continue to constitute one of the cornerstones of a transnational regulation of arbitration.

51. Efforts to develop transnational rules for the various problems are therefore very much to be welcomed and encouraged, rather than opposed.

An interesting example of other efforts at developing such rules are the IBA "Guidelines Party on Party Representation in International Arbitration", which seek to lay down certain ethical rules applicable to party representatives in arbitral proceedings. In my view [31], this instrument is a very worthwhile endeavor, because the rules on the ethics and conduct of counsel vary widely across legal systems and cultures. The application of domestic rules to these issues leads to significant complications in international proceedings involving counsel from different jurisdictions who may find themselves subject to different regimes, with negative consequences on the arbitration.

Nonetheless these Guidelines have been criticized for a variety of reasons, mainly on the grounds that the rules prevailing in different systems are too different and engrained in national traditions and cultures, that there are a variety of interests involved, including public ones, and that national rules on the subject are mandatory. Instead, although they are a useful starting point, on a proper analysis they are actually too tame and toothless. This is partly due precisely to the fact that the Guidelines are premised on the assumption that many of the issues that they attempt to tackle are governed by mandatory domestic rules (those governing the conduct of lawyers). In my opinion, however, if such rules are examined carefully and considering their

30. See for example T. Landau's well known criticism, in particular, "Tainted Memories: Exposing the Fallacy of Witness Evidence in International Arbitration", Fourth Kaplan Lecture at the Hong Kong Internatonal Arbitration Centre, 2010; "You would be Shocked: A Fireside Chat with Toby Landau", in *Global Arbitration Review*, 2021; "Is it Time for a Rethink?", in *Global Arbitration Review*, 2022.

31. See L. G. Radicati di Brozolo and Flavio Ponzano, "The Need for Arbitration-Specific Rules on Ethics", note 15 above.

original scope of application, it is easy to conclude that they do not prevent a uniform regulation of the activities of lawyers in international arbitrations, in keeping with the needs of these proceedings. As a matter of fact, the disparities and inequalities inherent in the application of those rules to international arbitration have the effect of prejudicing some of the parties they are intended to protect when they are applied in their original domestic context, where all parties play on a level field.

The same could be said for privilege, which is an equally thorny issue, but for which there is at the moment no equivalent attempt to develop transnational rules fit for arbitration.

52. Another important attempt at developing transnational rules are the ILA Recommendations on *res judicata* which propose an arbitration-specific solution for the important issue of the preclusive effects of arbitral awards. These too have been the object of misdirected criticism, based primarily on the fact that the solutions envisaged by them do not reflect a shared approach to *res judicata* across domestic legal systems, which on this subject vary considerably. It is on the basis of this consideration that several arbitral tribunals and national courts have refused to consider these Recommendations and fallen back on a rather pedantic and insufficiently reflected application of domestic law. This solution first of all ignores that the differences on this subject between domestic legal systems are not as extreme as usually assumed [32]. Perhaps even more importantly, it ignores that domestic rules on *res judicata* have developed for domestic judgments, which pose different problems to arbitral awards, and that particularly those of civil law jurisdictions are not suited for arbitration, given their restrictive and formalistic approach. It also overlooks that, if the issue is considered in depth and giving due consideration to the peculiarities of arbitration and the differences with domestic *res judicata*, there is little basis to view domestic rules as mandatory, at least in the sense that they do not prevent giving broad preclusive effects to prior awards [33].

The ILA Recommendations set out a well-reasoned and structured set of principles on the preclusive effect to be recognized to arbitral

---

32. See C. Chainais, "L'autorité de la chose jugée en procédure civile: perspectives de droit comparé", *Revue de l'Arbitrage*, 2016, p. 3 *et seq*.

33. For some further reflections see L. G. Radicati di Brozolo, "What Rules must International Arbitrators apply to Decide According to the Law?", forthcoming in *Arbitration International*, 2023. These issues are also the subject of an in-depth analysis in a forthcoming article of mine on *res judicata* in international arbitration.

awards, very much in keeping with the spirit and goals of arbitration for which the finality of the decision of disputes is crucial. These principles commend themselves both to arbitrators and to courts and provide a solid basis for a transnational solution and for not resorting to domestic law. The Recommendations, like other soft law instruments, are good examples of how creative thinking and an understanding of the peculiarities of international arbitration, unhindered by the belief of the need for a passive adherence to domestic law, can lead to the elaboration of the uniform arbitration-specific rules that are essential for a proper functioning of arbitration.

53. The international arbitral community should therefore become more proactive in developing instruments of this sort for the many problems for which accepted transnational solutions have not yet emerged. Given the complexity of the rule-making process within organizations such as the IBA and the ILA, I have advocated that arbitral institutions should assume a greater role in this process by including in their rules solutions for some of the relevant issues, at least those that can be disposed of by the parties. The rules adopted by arbitral institutions would be applicable on a contractual basis, avoiding the complex task of determining whether existing transnational solutions are available. At the same time, those rules would not impinge on the flexibility of arbitration and the freedom of the parties, since they could be framed as default rules applicable in the absence of a different agreement of the parties. This may not lead to uniformity, because the various institutions could adopt different solutions for the same problems, but it would offer the parties the choice to different alternatives. Alternatively, since arbitral institutions compete to offer the best rules, the competition could lead to convergence in a relatively reduced timeframe.

CHAPTER VII

CONCLUSION: THE REDUCTION OF THE ROLE OF DOMESTIC LAW IN FAVOR OF UNIFORM ARBITRATION-SPECIFIC RULES IS ESSENTIAL TO ENHANCE ARBITRATION'S EFFECTIVENESS

54. The theme of this lecture intended to honor the memory of Emmanuel Gaillard has been the need to counter the tendency of arbitration practitioners and national courts alike to rely unnecessarily on domestic law when tackling arbitration-related problems, and to show the need for transnational solutions in keeping with the spirit and needs of international arbitration.

55. The recourse to domestic law (which presupposes the recourse to conflict of laws) for arbitration-related issues other than the merits is a source of uncertainty and lack of uniformity and often precludes solutions specifically suited for arbitration. It is starkly at odds with what arbitration should aspire to be in order to fulfill the expectations of its users, who seek a truly uniform and predictable system of transnational justice that provides solutions tailored to its peculiarities and not randomly elaborated by individual domestic systems or copy-pasted from domestic civil procedure.

56. It is for example inconceivable that a dispute-settlement mechanism that ought to be responsive to those needs can be plagued by the uncertainties that still prevail on fundamental matters such as, for instance, the law governing arbitration agreements, which impacts on the foreseeability of the rules that will be applied to determine the validity and effects of such agreements, and that the rules on these issues vary from one domestic system to the other. It is equally inconceivable, to mention another example, that the preclusive effects of arbitral awards can vary haphazardly depending on whether the rules of one system are applied rather than those of another.

57. The need for uniform arbitration-specific solutions is consistent with Emmanuel Gaillard's vision of international arbitration centered on his notion of arbitral legal order. This notion, which is pragmatic rather than dogmatic, does not deny the authority of domestic legal systems over arbitration. Instead, it essentially takes stock, on the one hand, of the relative freedom that those systems accord

to arbitration, without insisting on the application of their rules within arbitral proceedings and allowing the emergence of uniform arbitration-specific rules; and, on the other hand, of a trend towards convergence of domestic legal systems on a range of issues and on the fact that there is room for a more flexible application of some of their rules which may permit further convergence and uniformity.

That vision is therefore important because it highlights the importance of the complex of principles and rules consisting of the core of common principles and approaches that can be gleaned from a comparison of the domestic rules of individual legal systems, as well as of the transnational rules and practices that prevail in the arbitration world. This body of rules is already capable of forming the basis for the decisions on a number of arbitration-related issues not only by arbitral tribunals, but also by national courts, in lieu of, and more appropriately than, domestic rules. Perhaps less controversially and to assuage the concerns of dogmatists over the use of the concept of arbitral *legal order*, this aggregate of rules may more simply be termed a uniform law of international arbitration.

58. Of course, that uniform law is still embryonic. Nonetheless, the recognition of its existence introduces an important change of perspective on the rules applicable to and in international arbitration. First, it spotlights the fact that there are alternatives to the pure and simple parochial application of domestic law (whether directly or via conflicts of law) which foster uniform and focused solutions to arbitration-related issues. It also increases the awareness of the benefits and need for such solutions. In turn, this should stimulate the development of appropriate approaches to issues beyond the ones that are the subject of existing transnational rules and the convergent approaches of individual domestic laws. By arbitrators, that can be achieved through the quest for *ad hoc* solutions they can identify through the exercise of their inherent powers or by following persuasive arbitral precedents. By courts, it can often (although not invariably) be achieved through constructive interpretations of their laws that favor their alignment with arbitral practice and any solutions of other domestic laws that may be more in line with the needs of arbitration.

The most significant impetus towards the elaboration of transnational rules for arbitration must however come from soft law instruments, such as those of the IBA and other institutions. As explained [34], there is

34. See para. 50 above.

no serious ground for opposing this type of rule-making, which should actually be highly encouraged because it is more efficient, faster and conducive to more certainty without jeopardizing flexibility, than the emergence of spontaneous rules from arbitral practice and case-law. Arbitral institutions should become more pro-active in these efforts They are the ones best placed to take on the task because they do not need to seek as broad a consensus as institutions like the IBA, and their rules could be made binding, subject to opt-out by the parties.

59. In sum, the proper development of arbitration to satisfy its ambition to offer users a uniform, predictable and well-functioning system of transnational justice requires abandoning the tendency, still so common to courts and arbitrators, to rely indiscriminately on domestic law, which compromises arbitration's proper functioning. Conversely, it requires the recourse by both judges and arbitrators to transnational solutions based on uniform, sufficiently precise but flexible arbitration-specific rules developed *ad hoc* for arbitration that in part already exist and in part still need to be elaborated. This body of rules, which is Gaillard's arbitral legal order or a uniform law of international arbitration, amounts to the applicable law to issues of arbitration not only when they arise in arbitration, but also when they arise before courts, as an alternative to and to the exclusion of domestic law.

60. Finally, the development of transnational rules would have another very significant advantage. If applied consistently within arbitral proceedings, those rules would make the mechanism more uniform and predictable and would contribute to upholding and enhancing the legitimacy and inclusivity of arbitration as an institution, consolidating the perception, by both States and users, that it is a mechanism governed by transparent and well-established common rules apt to ensure its optimal functioning.

61. Emmanuel Gaillard's theorization of the legal framework of international arbitration provides a powerful impetus for a fruitful recalibration of the relationship between arbitration and domestic rules, without subverting the fundamental role of domestic law. It is a great loss that he did not have the opportunity to elaborate further on this theme in the General Course he was due to deliver at this Academy in 2022.

NATIONAL LEGAL ORDERS AND ARBITRAL LEGAL ORDER: CONFLICT OR COORDINATION?

by

Yas Banifatemi [1]

2022 was the much-awaited year when Professor Emmanuel Gaillard was set to inaugurate the three-week General Course format in private international law at The Hague Academy, delivering a General Course on "The New Theory of Conflicts of Systems: National Legal Orders and Arbitral Legal Order" ("La nouvelle théorie des conflits des ordres : ordres juridiques étatiques et ordre juridique arbitral").

By taking the angle of the interaction between legal systems, and although taking as his starting point the traditional private international law concepts of conflicts of norms and conflicts of jurisdictions, Professor Gaillard had set for himself the ambition of reconsidering the entirety of the field of private international law through the prism of international arbitration law. Sadly, we will never know how much he would have, yet again, revolutionized both fields, but we do know that the extremely rich doctrinal work that Professor Gaillard has left for us will suffice to keep generations of scholars busy in the decades to come.

In choosing a closely related topic for this tribute, and treating it somewhat differently, I certainly have not taken the easy path. In fact, and referring to the French meaning of "lecture" (*"lecture"* or "reading"), I simply could have read for you excerpts of any of Professor Gaillard's many writings on the subject – indeed I have chosen to heavily refer to those writings, in English or in French, given the refinement of his thinking and an eloquence that has remained and will remain unparalleled:

– Of course, I will refer to his seminal book on the Legal Theory of International Arbitration *(Aspects philosophiques du droit de*

1. Yas Banifatemi is a founding partner of Gaillard Banifatemi Shelbaya Disputes. She is also the President of the International Arbitration Institute (IAI), having succeeded the late Professor Gaillard in that capacity. She practices international arbitration as counsel, arbitrator and expert. She teaches at Yale Law School, Harvard Law School, Panthéon-Sorbonne University and the Sciences Po School of Law, and researches in the areas of international arbitration and public international law.

l'arbitrage international), published in 2008 in the French version and in 2010 in the English version [2].

- I will also refer to his 2013 article on "Transcending National Legal Orders for International Arbitration" [3].
- I will discuss in more detail his ground-breaking study of 2018 titled "Coordination or Chaos: Do the Principles of Comity, *Lis Pendens*, and *Res Judicata* Apply to International Arbitration?" [4].
- I will also refer to the lecture that Professor Gaillard gave, that same year, in Pierre Lalive's honor, "The Myth of Harmony in International Arbitration" [5].
- I will examine, again from that same year, his article on "Dialogue des ordres juridiques: ordre juridique arbitral et ordres juridiques étatiques" [6].
- I will further refer to an article from 2020 on "The Arbitral Legal Order: Evolution and Recognition" [7].

Conflict, coordination, chaos, harmony. For those who knew Professor Gaillard, it is no surprise that, at the apex of his career and scholarly work, and having conceived a number of fundamental concepts of international arbitration – among them, the negative effect of competence-competence, the notion of representation of international arbitration, the concept of the arbitral legal order, or that of abuse of process in international arbitration – he was further pursuing his thinking into the systemic aspects of international arbitration.

We will have the luxury of hearing the Course that will be taught by Judge Dominique Hascher on the extent to which national courts' decisions reflect one of the three "representations" of international

---

2. E. Gaillard, *Legal Theory of International Arbitration*, Martinus Nijhoff Publishers, 2010; E. Gaillard, "Aspects philosophiques du droit de l'arbitrage international", *Recueil des cours*, Vol. 329 (2007), pp. 49-216; also available in the Academy's pocket book collection; ADI-Poche (2008).

3. E. Gaillard, "Transcending National Legal Orders for International Arbitration", *International Arbitration: The Coming of a New Age?, ICCA Congress Series No. 17*, 2013, pp. 371 *et seq*.

4. E. Gaillard, "Coordination or Chaos: Do the Principles of Comity, *Lis Pendens*, and *Res Judicata* Apply to International Arbitration?", *The American Review of International Arbitration*, Vol. 29, No. 3, 2018, pp. 205 *et seq*.

5. E. Gaillard, "The Myth of Harmony in International Arbitration", *ICSID Review – Foreign Investment Law Journal*, Vol. 34, Issue 3, 2019, pp. 553 *et seq*.

6. E. Gaillard, "Dialogue des ordres juridiques: ordre juridique arbitral et ordres juridiques étatiques", *Revue de l'arbitrage*, 2018, pp. 493 *et seq*.

7. E. Gaillard, "The Arbitral Legal Order: Evolution and Recognition", in *The Oxford Handbook of International Arbitration*, T. Schultz and F. Ortino (eds.), Oxford University Press, 2020, pp. 554 *et seq*.

arbitration, which is perhaps the most important concept conceived by Professor Gaillard in his Legal Theory of International Arbitration and presented at this very place, The Hague Academy of International Law, in 2007. It is precisely because of the constant back-and-forth between international arbitration and national legal orders, mostly through national courts – be it, to take just a few examples, in relation to referrals to arbitration, the determination of the existence and validity of an arbitration agreement (on a *prima facie* basis or not), the assistance provided in the constitution of an arbitral tribunal or in evidentiary matters, and setting aside or enforcement proceedings – that Professor Gaillard explored the concept of the "dialogue" between legal orders. The question, then, is whether that dialogue is constructive, cooperative, or whether it takes place at cross purposes (in French, I would refer to a *"dialogue de sourds"*). The answer to this question lies in how national legal orders perceive – in Professor Gaillard's terminology, "represent" – international arbitration.

CHAPTER I

THE COEXISTENCE OF AN ARBITRAL LEGAL ORDER ALONGSIDE NATIONAL LEGAL ORDERS

The question of "National Legal Orders and Arbitral Legal Order: Conflict or Coordination?" naturally assumes that there is such a thing as an arbitral legal order.

Is one to find the source of legitimacy and adjudicatory power of arbitrators in State-based law, that of the various national legal orders around the world? If yes, would that be restricted to the law of the State in which the parties or the tribunal have fixed the seat of the arbitration? Is it to be found in party autonomy? But then, what grounds the parties' authority to grant adjudicatory power to the arbitrators? As Professor Gaillard put it in his Hague Course of 2007,

> "the arbitrators' power to render a decision, which is private in nature, on the basis of an equally private agreement of the parties, begs a fundamental question. Where does the source of such power and the legal nature of the process and of the ensuing decision stem from? This question may be referred to as that of the 'juridicity' of international arbitration" [8].

He further observed that "the contractual nature of arbitration could not, in itself, resolve the fundamental question of the source of validity of the agreement from which arbitrators derive their power to adjudicate" [9]. One sees that the old debate on the judicial or contractual nature of arbitration was not and could not be satisfactory; nor could the other debate over the distinction between the territorial and contractual approaches to international arbitration be any more productive.

These observations led Professor Gaillard to search for "[o]nly those conceptions that can account for the entire phenomenon of international arbitration, its sources, its objectives and its structures" [10]. Naturally, there is no better way to summarize those conceptions – or, more accurately, subconscious mental representations of the field [11] – than

8. E. Gaillard, *Legal Theory of International Arbitration*, *op. cit.*, para. 2.
9. *Ibid.*, para. 9.
10. *Ibid.*, para. 10.
11. On the subconscious aspect of the representations, see E. Gaillard, "The Representations of International Arbitration", *Journal of International Dispute Settlement*, 2010, pp. 5-6.

to refer directly to Professor Gaillard, in his article on "Transcending National Legal Orders for International Arbitration":

> "There are three competing visions of international arbitration, which structure the way in which one thinks about international arbitration. These visions, mental constructs, or representations reflect what their proponents consider to be the source of legitimacy of international arbitration, namely the source of the arbitrator's power to adjudicate.
>
> The first and most traditional view is what can be characterized as the 'monolocal' representation. It is a territorialist view that considers the *law of the seat* of the arbitration to be the *sole source* of legitimacy and validity of the arbitral process. In this vision, the seat of the arbitration is more than a location chosen for convenience or neutrality; it provides the exclusive basis for the power of the arbitrators to adjudicate and produce an arbitral award, which will bear the 'nationality' of the seat of the arbitration. Accordingly, the courts of the seat of the arbitration are given wide latitude to determine the extent of their involvement in the arbitral process, and proponents of the territorialist view consider the decisions rendered by those courts to be binding internationally. In this vision, international arbitration does not transcend national legal orders; to the contrary, it concentrates the source of validity and legitimacy of the arbitral process in one national system, that of the seat of the arbitration.
>
> The second vision is the 'Westphalian' representation, a model in which each state decides for itself the conditions under which it will consider an arbitral process to be legitimate and the resulting award worthy of recognition. Because this vision legitimizes the arbitral process *a posteriori*, namely if an award meets the enforcing State's criteria, the seat of the arbitration is not of ultimate importance. Unlike the territorialist view, the Westphalian vision considers that international arbitration can derive its legitimacy from a *plurality of legal systems*, namely various States of enforcement. However, the Westphalian vision does not transcend national legal orders any more than the territorialist vision; it simply allocates differently the source of validity and legitimacy of international arbitration amongst various individual national legal orders.
>
> Only the third vision, which truly constitutes the 'transnational' representation, accepts that international arbitration transcends

national legal orders and that it constitutes a transnational system of justice sometimes labeled as the 'arbitral legal order'. Importantly, national legal systems are not excluded from this transnational legal order, but the arbitral process no longer hinges on the particularities of the national legal order at the seat of the arbitration or elsewhere. Instead, this vision recognizes that the validity and legitimacy of international arbitration is rooted in the *collectivity of national legal orders*, as opposed to one or even several individual national legal systems. In other words, the arbitral legal order incorporates and reflects the trends stemming from national legal systems." [12]

As this excerpt makes clear, Professor Gaillard was very much a positivist – and we will hear Professor Fernández Arroyo tell us more this week about "Emmanuel Gaillard, the positivist": never departing from the national legal orders as the source of legitimacy of international arbitration and, thus, the source of the arbitrators' power to adjudicate. Simply, the difference in the three visions, or mental representations of the field, lies in the belief that such a source comes from one State only (*i.e.*, that of the seat of the arbitration), from a plurality of States depending on the parties' election as to where they will seek enforcement of their award, or from the collectivity of States acting together [13].

As regards the transnational representation of international arbitration in particular, Professor Gaillard explained in his Legal Theory of International Arbitration that this philosophy was rooted in the normative activity of States:

> "The representation that accepts the existence of an arbitral legal order reflects a very different ideology. Far from stigmatizing the alleged inadequacy of national laws, it *relies on the notion that the laws of various States*, when considered *collectively*, make up the common rules of arbitration law in which the source of the arbitrators' power to adjudicate is rooted. Like general principles of law, which constitute one of the sources of international law, this representation is *not defined in opposition to national*

12. E. Gaillard, "Transcending National Legal Orders for International Arbitration", *op. cit.*, pp. 372-373 (emphasis added).

13. For a discussion of the jusnaturalist approach of the transnational view, see E. Gaillard, "The Arbitral Legal Order: Evolution and Recognition", *op. cit.*, p. 558.

> *laws*. Rather, it is entirely *based* on the normative activity of States." [14]

He even went further on the transnational legal order's foundation on national legal systems, explaining in his article on "Transcending National Legal Orders for International Arbitration":

> "Transcending national legal orders is therefore not synonymous with the creation of an a-national legal order, which would be characterized by a rejection of, or opposition to, national legal systems. To the contrary, the transnational view of international arbitration is a vision that *embraces rather than rejects the laws derived from national legal systems*, acknowledging and following *trends developed collectively by national legal systems*. Thus, the transnational vision recognizes an arbitral legal order that is *founded on national legal systems*, while at the same time transcending any individual national legal order." [15]

Professor Gaillard also showed in his study on "The Arbitral Legal Order: Evolution and Recognition" that, beyond being a mental construct, the arbitral legal order exists "as a system of law", recognized by national legal orders, arbitral institutions and arbitrators themselves [16]. He also explained how it is an organized body of norms containing its own sources, performing its functions through its own organs, and ensuring true effectiveness ("un ensemble organisé de normes possédant un système de sources qui lui est propre, des organes que sont les arbitres, et un degré d'effectivité qui n'a rien à envier à celui des ordres juridiques étatiques") [17].

Given that each of these three representations, or mental constructs, that each person intuitively espouses about international arbitration – be it an arbitrator, counsel, or a national judge – structures a given

---

14. E. Gaillard, *Legal Theory of International Arbitration*, *op. cit.*, para. 53 (emphasis added).

15. E. Gaillard, "Transcending National Legal Orders for International Arbitration", *op. cit.*, p. 373 (emphasis added). See also E. Gaillard, "International Arbitration as a Transnational System of Justice", *Arbitration – The Next Fifty Years*, *ICCA Congress Series No. 16*, 2012, pp. 68-69.

16. E. Gaillard, "The Arbitral Legal Order: Evolution and Recognition", *op. cit.*, p. 568.

17. E. Gaillard, "Dialogue des ordres juridiques: ordre juridique arbitral et ordres juridiques étatiques", *op. cit.*, p. 495. See also the John E. C. Brierly Commemorative Conference given by Prof. Gaillard on 24 September 2009, E. Gaillard, "L'ordre juridique arbitral: réalité, utilité et spécificité", *McGill Law Journal*, Vol. 55, 2010, p. 896.

individual's approach to the field in its entirety, it is no surprise that these representations have an impact on the interplay between international arbitration and national legal systems. As also explained by Professor Gaillard in that same study,

> "a representation offers a comprehensive mental construct of the *fundamental relationship between a national legal system and international arbitration* which serves as a source of legitimacy and validity of international arbitration" [18].

But no one needs to embrace the concept of an arbitral legal order to understand the coexistence between international arbitration and national legal systems, and the interaction between the two. In other words, because international arbitration, as a phenomenon, is perceived in each of these representations in a different manner, this mental perception will have an impact on the way in which arbitrators – and, beyond them, arbitration law itself – will interact with national legal orders, and vice versa.

Let us conclude on this mark with Professor Gaillard's own words in his article on "Dialogue des ordres juridiques: ordre juridique arbitral et ordres juridiques étatiques":

> "L'évocation d'un dialogue entre l'ordre juridique arbitral et les ordres juridiques étatiques est l'occasion de rappeler que le droit de l'arbitrage n'est pas l'apanage exclusif de l'ordre juridique arbitral. Lorsque la Cour de cassation française reconnaît dans l'arbitre un juge international, ou évoque l'existence d'un ordre juridique arbitral dont la pierre angulaire est la Convention de New York, le juge français ne devient pas l'organe de l'ordre juridique arbitral. Il demeure celui de l'ordre juridique français dont la tâche est d'accueillir, ou non, la sentence dans cet ordre juridique. Pour ne prendre qu'un exemple, l'ordre public international qu'il contrôle est la conception française de l'ordre public international, l'ordre public 'véritablement international' étant celui des arbitres. On se trouve en présence d'un *dialogue* des ordres juridiques, *non d'une confusion* des ordres juridiques." [19]

---

18. E. Gaillard, "The Arbitral Legal Order: Evolution and Recognition", *op. cit.*, p. 554 (emphasis added).

19. E. Gaillard, "Dialogue des ordres juridiques: ordre juridique arbitral et ordres juridiques étatiques", *op. cit.*, p. 495 (emphasis added).

CHAPTER II

CONFLICT OR COORDINATION: PRACTICAL EFFECTS OF THE REPRESENTATIONS OF INTERNATIONAL ARBITRATION

In his remarkable 2018 study on "Coordination or Chaos", in which he focused on comity as a "source principle" and the "key coordination mechanisms" of *lis pendens*, anti-suit injunctions, and *res judicata* [20], Professor Gaillard outlined three ways in which a dialogue – be it harmonious or conflicting – is engaged between national legal orders and the arbitral legal order: coordination among national courts and arbitral tribunals, coordination among arbitral tribunals themselves, and coordination among national courts *about* arbitration. The first type of interaction, which is the focus of today's lecture, is therefore far from exhausting the subject.

I will address two specific examples of what I believe exemplifies the acid test of the interaction between legal orders. The first is the negative effect of competence-competence as a *coordination* benchmark for establishing jurisdiction; the second is the anti-suit injunction as an instrument of *conflict* in the arbitrators' exercise of their adjudicatory power. In each instance, as in every other instance in the life of an arbitration, the confrontation between legal orders results in coordination or conflict depending on the representation of international arbitration that is adopted – consciously or subconsciously – by the relevant actor, namely the national judge and the arbitrator.

I will not address, for lack of time, the post-award process, namely the question of the effect of the annulment of an arbitral award in the country of the seat, as this question may concern more specifically the coordination among national courts *about* arbitration. In other words, this concerns the question whether courts in a given country are expected, for enforcement purposes, to review and give effect to the arbitral award itself even if it has been set aside at the seat of the arbitration, or whether they are called to make a determination about other courts' decision(s) *about* the award. Professor Gaillard, consistent

20. E. Gaillard, "Coordination or Chaos: Do the Principles of Comity, *Lis Pendens*, and *Res Judicata* Apply to International Arbitration?", *op. cit.*, pp. 206- 207.

with the text and philosophy of the 1958 New York Convention [21], as well as the French courts' long-standing approach, took the strong view that the subject of the review of an enforcement court must be the award itself, notwithstanding the fate of the award in any country, including that of the seat of the arbitration. That said, this question too is another acid test for the interaction between national legal systems and the arbitral legal order, as it determines whether national courts are willing to view an arbitral award as the product of a distinct system of justice, or whether they view it as a product that is subject to the green or red lights given, more or less randomly, by other national courts. In this relation Professor Gaillard relied on the coordination concept of *res judicata* in his article on "Coordination or Chaos":

> "[t]he res judicata effect of an international arbitral award flows directly from the New York Convention, which, in eliminating the double exequatur requirement that previously existed under the 1927 Geneva Convention, requires Contracting States to 'recognize arbitral awards as binding and enforce them,' subject to the conditions laid down in the Convention" [22].

---

21. See E. Gaillard, "The Enforcement of Awards Set Aside in the Country of Origin", *ICSID Review – Foreign Investment Law Journal*, 1999, pp. 32 *et seq.*; E. Gaillard, "The Relationship of the New York Convention with Other Treaties and with Domestic Law", in *Enforcement of Arbitration Agreements and International Arbitral Awards*, E. Gaillard and D. Di Pietro (eds.), Cameron May, 2008, pp. 85-87; E. Gaillard, "The Urgency of Not Revising the New York Convention", *50 Years of the New York Convention, ICCA Congress Series No. 14*, 2009, pp. 695-696; E. Gaillard, "International Arbitration as a Transnational System of Justice", *op. cit.*, pp. 71-73; E. Gaillard, "La vision américaine des sentences annulées au siège sur les arrêts *Pemex* et *Thaï-Lao Lignite*", note sous Cour d'appel des Etats-Unis, 2e circuit, 2 août 2016 et 20 juillet 2017", *Revue de l'arbitrage*, 2017, pp. 1147 *et seq*; E. Gaillard, "Coordination or Chaos: Do the Principles of Comity, *Lis Pendens*, and *Res Judicata* Apply to International?", *op. cit.*, pp. 238-239, 241-242; E. Gaillard, "The Myth of Harmony in International Arbitration", *op. cit.*, p. 564 ("The approach focusing on the preclusive effect of court decisions ancillary to the award, as opposed to scrutiny of the award itself, creates an opening for opportunistic parties to manipulate the system. In particular, it invites parties to race to the court expected to be most sympathetic to their position, in the hope of securing a favorable judgment, which can then be exported to other countries. In my view, harmony is better fostered by going back to the logic of the New York Convention, namely that national courts at the place (or places) of enforcement should independently assess the arbitral process and the ensuing award, irrespective of the assessment by the courts of any other country. In fact, the State of enforcement of the award has a strong interest in ensuring that the award meets the standards of what it considers to be a decision worthy of recognition, according to the rules applicable to enforcement in that country"). See also UNCITRAL Secretariat Guide on the Convention on the Recognition and Enforcement of Foreign Arbitral Awards (New York, 1958), 2016, authored by Professor Emmanuel Gaillard, along with the UNCITRAL Secretariat, available on www.newyorkconvention1958.org.

22. E. Gaillard, "Coordination or Chaos: Do the Principles of Comity, *Lis Pendens*, and *Res Judicata* Apply to International Arbitration?", *op. cit.*, p. 219.

A. Establishing jurisdiction: the negative effect of competence-competence as a coordination benchmark

The question of the jurisdiction of arbitrators is one of the first questions that comes to mind when considering the relationship between legal orders. Who decides jurisdiction [23]? The arbitrator or the national judge? If the latter, which judge? The rule of competence-competence, a well-established substantive rule of international arbitration [24], teaches us that it is, and should be, the arbitrator. Just as national or international courts are entitled to rule on their own jurisdiction, international arbitration law has adopted this concept to empower arbitrators to rule on their own jurisdiction. As explained in the article that I had the honor of co-writing with Professor Gaillard on the "Rule of Priority", there is no "illogicality" arising from the fact that arbitral tribunals are not permanent bodies and that the determination of their jurisdiction is "founded on the parties' agreement, which [they] may eventually find to be inexistent or vitiated, to arbitrate their dispute" [25]. The whole premise of the principle of competence-competence, here expressed in its so-called positive effect – an expression coined by Professor Gaillard – is that arbitrators can be trusted to rule on their own jurisdiction. But that is not the end of the inquiry: what happens when the recalcitrant party, wanting to avoid the arbitration, brings the dispute (including on its merits) before a national court? If one were to respect both the arbitration agreement and the arbitrators' power to determine their own jurisdiction, the principle of competence-competence would entail that the court that is seized of the dispute and the question of the validity and effect of the arbitration agreement should not, in parallel and with the same degree of scrutiny, rule on those issues, at least at the outset of the arbitral process and subject to a *prima facie* determination that the agreement to arbitrate is not "null and void, inoperative or incapable of being performed". This principle,

---

23. On this question, see also the 2022 Gaillard Debate of the Arbitration Academy on "The Arbitrator's Jurisdiction: Who Decides?", between Professor G. Bermann and Y. Banifatemi, available on the website of the Arbitration Academy: https://arbitrationacademy.org/2022-emmanuel-gaillard-debate/.

24. On the substantive rules of international arbitration, see E. Gaillard, "Les vertus de la méthode des règles matérielles appliquées à la convention d'arbitrage (les enseignements de l'affaire *Kout Food*)", *Revue de l'arbitrage*, 2020, pp. 716-717.

25. E. Gaillard and Y. Banifatemi, "Negative Effect of Competence-Competence: The Rule of Priority in Favour of the Arbitrators", *Enforcement of Arbitration Agreements and International Arbitral Awards*, E. Gaillard and D. Di Pietro (eds.), Cameron May, 2008, p. 259.

known as the "negative effect" of competence-competence and also coined by Professor Gaillard, essentially means that the arbitrators must be the *first*, as opposed to the *sole*, judges of their own jurisdiction, with possible court review at the stage of any enforcement or setting aside action [26]. This is entirely consistent with Article II (3) of the 1958 New York Convention on the Recognition and Enforcement of Foreign Arbitral Awards, which provides:

> "The court of a Contracting State, when seized of an action in a matter in respect of which the parties have made an agreement within the meaning of this article, *shall*, at the request of one of the parties, *refer the parties to arbitration*, unless it finds that the said agreement is null and void, inoperative or incapable of being performed."

When the principle is fully given effect, the relationship between legal orders is harmonious, coordinated, and trustful. As explained by Professor Gaillard repeatedly, and again in his article on "Dialogue des ordres juridiques: ordre juridique arbitral et ordres juridiques étatiques", this is ultimately a test of the pro-arbitration bias adopted by a legal system: "On peut … voir dans l'acceptation de la règle l'un des révélateurs essentiels du degré de faveur qu'un ordre juridique étatique est prêt à consentir à l'arbitrage" [27]. This is the case in numerous countries in Europe, Latin America, Africa and Asia.

One well-known example is the 2015 *Tomolugen Holdings* decision in Singapore, in which the Court of Appeal held:

> ". . . to require the court, on a stay application under s. 6 of the IAA, to undertake a full determination of an arbitral tribunal's jurisdiction could significantly hollow the kompetenz-kompetenz principle of its practical effect. The full merits approach has the potential to reduce an arbitral tribunal's kompetenz-kompetenz to a contingency dependent on the strategic choices of the claimant in a putative arbitration. If the claimant decides to pursue its claim by arbitration, the arbitral tribunal will determine any challenge to its jurisdiction, and thus, its kompetenz-kompetenz will be given full vent. But, if the claimant decides to pursue its

26. *Ibid.*, pp. 259-260. See also E. Gaillard, "Actualité de l'effet négatif de la compétence-compétence", in *Mélanges en l'honneur du Professeur Bertrand Ancel*, 2018, p. 680.

27. Emmanuel Gaillard, "Dialogue des ordres juridiques: ordre juridique arbitral et ordres juridiques étatiques", *op. cit.*, p. 497.

claim by bringing proceedings in court (instead of by recourse to arbitration), the court will be seized of jurisdiction, and will be able (and, indeed, on the full merits approach, obliged) to make a full determination on the existence and scope of the arbitration clause; this will deprive the putative arbitral tribunal of its kompetenz-kompetenz." [28]

A similar reasoning had been adopted in 2007 by the Hong Kong Court of Appeal in *PCCW*, when it emphasized that "[i]t is important for the court *not to usurp* the function of the arbitrators, and unless . . . [the tribunal's lack of jurisdiction] is clear, the matter should be stayed for arbitration" [29].

By contrast, one may query to what extent the law in the United States consistently supports international arbitration. As Professor Gaillard explains in his article on "Coordination or Chaos", in the main decision on the subject, *First Options of Chicago* v. *Kaplan*, the United States Supreme Court

> "rejected the principle of competence-competence and instead established a presumption that parties to an arbitration agreement have not agreed to arbitrate the issues of existence and validity of the arbitration agreement unless there is 'clear and unmistakable' evidence to the contrary" [30].

Notwithstanding that a number of appellate courts in the US have protected the principle of competence-competence by finding, for example, that the reference to arbitration rules (ICC or UNCITRAL, for example) in the arbitration agreement marks the parties' clear and unmistakable intention to submit to the arbitrators the determination of the existence and validity of the arbitration agreement, the law in the US remains uncertain, especially if one considers the additional layer of the so-called "gateway issues". In the vision of Professor George Bermann, who has championed this concept, this concerns "the allocation between courts and arbitrators of competence to determine threshold issues in arbitration" and that "courts be allowed to treat certain threshold issues as gateway issues, and address them if asked

28. *Tomolugen Holdings Ltd* v. *Silica Investors Ltd.* [2015], SGCA 57, para. 67.
29. *PCCW Glob. Ltd.* v. *Interactive Comm'ns Serv. Ltd.* [2007], 1 HKLRD 309, para. 60 (CA) (emphasis added).
30. E. Gaillard, "Coordination or Chaos: Do the Principles of Comity, *Lis Pendens*, and *Res Judicata* Apply to International Arbitration?", *op. cit.*, p. 210.

to do so at the outset of arbitration" [31]. Professor Gaillard's response can be found in his article on "Consent: The Essence of an Ordinary Jurisdiction", based on a speech given in September 2016 at the Brazilian Arbitration Committee:

> "... the degree to which arbitration is considered as an exceptional, rather than ordinary, jurisdiction will inform how much courts seek to control the arbitration process *a priori*. Of particular relevance to this discussion is the practice of some courts, when seized of a matter covered by an arbitration agreement, to review the parties' consent to arbitrate in a detailed manner before the arbitrators have had the opportunity to do so. This practice persists even in jurisdictions generally favorable to arbitration. For instance, the US courts uphold a general pro-arbitration policy but have also adopted a practice of allocating certain jurisdictional 'gateway issues' for interlocutory judicial determination, before those issues are referred to the arbitrators. One prominent proponent of this approach paints the illustration of 'a 'portal' through which a party seeking arbitration must pass before arbitration may commence'. The conception that parties who have consented to arbitrate are required to pass through a 'portal' or 'gate' guarded by court judges, in order to reap the benefits of their arbitration agreement, evidences an unnecessary diffidence towards arbitration. ... [C]ourts in other jurisdictions have unequivocally affirmed their trust of international arbitration as an ordinary form of adjudication, and have rejected these types of measures aimed at controlling *a priori* the arbitral process" [32].

These examples show the extent to which the arbitration law principle of competence-competence, taken in both its positive and negative effects, is fully capable of resolving, in a harmonious manner, the interaction between arbitrators and national courts (and between the arbitral legal order and national legal orders) when it comes to the jurisdiction of arbitrators and their power to rule on their own jurisdiction.

31. G. Bermann, "The 'Gateway' Problem in International Commercial Arbitration", *Yale Journal of International Law*, 2012, pp. 49-50.

32. E. Gaillard, "Consent: The Essence of an Ordinary Jurisdiction", *Trabalhos do XV Congresso Internacional de Arbitragem – 2016 do Comitê Brasileiro de Arbitragem – CBAr: Consentimento na Arbitragem Internacional*, 2017, p. 7, at p. 21.

In that sense, and as shown by Professor Gaillard, coordination concepts that apply in the relationship between national courts, such as *lis pendens* and comity, are of little use in international arbitration. *Lis pendens* assumes that the two bodies that have been seized of the same dispute in sequence are equally competent to hear the dispute. As explained by Professor Gaillard in his article on "Coordination or Chaos",

> "[a]s between an arbitral tribunal and a court, however, the situation does not arise: the existence of a valid arbitration agreement conferring jurisdiction on an arbitral tribunal necessarily excludes the jurisdiction of national courts. In other words, either an arbitral tribunal will be exclusively competent over a dispute, or it will not be competent at all" [33].

Comity, for its part,

> "provides insufficient safeguard as it would subject arbitral jurisdiction to a case-by-case, discretionary willingness to allow arbitration to proceed, whereas arbitration involves a situation of a singular presumptively competent forum (the arbitral tribunal) as opposed to competing forums with plausible claims to jurisdiction" [34].

The rule-based approach adopted by arbitration law (or, in a transnational view, by the arbitral legal order) thus creates the conditions for greater predictability and harmony of solutions when it comes to matters of jurisdiction. It also disincentivizes parties from playing procedural games by rushing to a foreign court or inventing frivolous challenges to the arbitration agreement; conversely, the court system would not be exploited by recalcitrant parties to initiate parallel and duplicative proceedings for the sole purpose of interfering with the progress of the arbitration. Each actor has its clearly defined place: arbitrators remain the judges of their own jurisdiction in the first instance, while courts recover their power of full scrutiny at the end of the arbitral process after the award is rendered by the arbitral tribunal.

---

33. E. Gaillard, "Coordination or Chaos: Do the Principles of Comity, *Lis Pendens*, and *Res Judicata* Apply to International?", *op. cit.*, p. 208.
34. *Ibid.*, p. 211.

B. Contesting the arbitrators' adjudicatory power: anti-suit injunctions as an instrument of conflict

The phenomenon of anti-suit injunctions is not new. As early as 2005, Professor Gaillard had dedicated a full conference under the aegis of the International Arbitration Institute to what was then a new trend [35]. Mostly, anti-suit injunctions have been used by recalcitrant parties, who would generally rush to their own courts to seek assistance in forcing the other party to withdraw, or not initiate, arbitration proceedings. In that sense, anti-suit injunctions may go well beyond issues of jurisdiction, as they seek to deny in its entirety the arbitrators' power to adjudicate the dispute brought before them.

The situation is not limited to legal systems where local courts may be used by recalcitrant parties, for example State-owned companies, as was the case in *Petrobangla* before the Bangladeshi courts or in *Pertamina* before the Indonesian courts. Countries such as the US and England are leaning towards the recognition of a limited judicial power to enjoin international arbitration, which is not displaying the most harmonious approach to arbitration.

Thus, the United States Draft Restatement of the US Law of International Commercial Arbitration ("Draft Restatement") establishes a court's power to enjoin international arbitration proceedings in the following terms:

> "Para. 2-29 Availability of Anti-Arbitration Injunctions
>
> *A court may enjoin a party to an international arbitration proceeding from proceeding with an arbitration to the extent that:*
>
> *(a)* *The party seeking the injunction establishes a defense to the enforcement of the agreement . . .*; and
>
> *(b)* issuance of an injunction is appropriate after consideration of the following:
>
> (1) the seat of the arbitration;
>
> (2) whether circumstances exist that raise substantial and justifiable doubt about the integrity of the arbitration proceedings; and
>
> (3) other principles applied by the forum court in determining whether to grant injunctive relief."

35. E. Gaillard (ed.), *Anti-Suit Injunctions in International Arbitration, IAI Series on International Arbitration No. 2*, Juris Publishing, 2005.

As discussed, however, allowing a court to decide arbitral jurisdiction on the basis of a full (as opposed to a *prima facie*) review at the pre-award stage runs contrary to the negative effect of competence-competence.

In England, section 37 of the Senior Courts Act provides that the High Court is empowered to grant injunctions "in all cases in which it appears to the court to be just and convenient to do so"; this power may, however, be exercised only to grant an anti-arbitration injunction in "exceptional circumstances and with caution", for example, "where the applicant's legal and equitable rights have been infringed or threatened by a continuation of the arbitration or that its continuation will be vexatious, oppressive or unconscionable".

One might say that, in both cases, the availability of anti-arbitration injunctions is limited to exceptional circumstances. Be that as it may, the express provision of such a power for the courts creates a sword of Damocles over international arbitration proceedings and legitimizes their use more broadly, including in other countries less inclined towards arbitration and, to the contrary, more willing to "intervene illegitimately on behalf of their own nationals seeking to evade an arbitration agreement". In the interaction between national systems and international arbitration, therefore, justice would be better served by a rule *prohibiting* anti-arbitration injunctions in all circumstances. As further noted by Professor Gaillard in his study on "Coordination or Chaos", "[t]his would require any potential irregularities in arbitral procedure to be addressed in post-award proceedings, while protecting the integrity of arbitration from interventionist courts" [36].

As these examples show, the question, once again, comes down to the trust of a given national legal order (including its courts) in the arbitration system and its vision of international arbitration as a system of justice.

The flipside of this question is how *arbitrators* are expected to respond to anti-arbitration injunctions targeting them, especially when they are issued by the courts of the seat. Here again, the response lies in the arbitrators' representation of international arbitration. An arbitrator who views his or her adjudicatory power as being grounded in the legal system of the seat has no option but to relinquish his or her power; an arbitrator embracing a Westphalian or pluralistic approach will aim

---

36. E. Gaillard, "Coordination or Chaos: Do the Principles of Comity, *Lis Pendens*, and *Res Judicata* Apply to International Arbitration?", *op. cit.*, pp. 216-217.

at rendering an enforceable award – and thus ignoring the anti-suit injunction – by considering the countries in which his or her award may be sought to be enforced; an arbitrator who believes that his or her authority to adjudicate is sourced in the transnational legal order and the collective normative activity of States will not subject himself or herself to the legal order of the seat or even that of any particular enforcement place, and will likewise not give effect to the local anti-suit injunction.

Among the many examples of anti-arbitration injunctions, one is of particular relevance given this week's tribute to Professor Gaillard: the anti-arbitration injunction issued against the Tribunal he was chairing in the *Salini* v. *Ethiopia* arbitration. In that case, involving an ICC arbitration with a seat in Addis Ababa, the Tribunal decided, consistent with the applicable ICC Arbitration Rules that expressly provided for the possibility of conducting hearings at any location the Tribunal considered appropriate under the circumstances, that the hearing in which certain witnesses would be heard would take place in Paris, without prejudice to Addis Ababa being the seat of the arbitration. Considering this to be an illegitimate procedural decision, the Respondent first challenged (unsuccessfully) the arbitrators before the ICC International Court of Arbitration. Following that, it obtained an anti-suit injunction from the Federal Supreme Court of Ethiopia, which ordered the Tribunal to immediately stay the proceedings until such time as the Court had rendered a decision on the ICC's dismissal of the challenge to the arbitrators. On 7 December 2001, the Tribunal issued an award on jurisdiction and on the Respondent's request for a stay of the arbitration, finding that:

> " . . . an arbitral tribunal constituted in such circumstances has a discretion as to whether or not it should comply with such an order. An international arbitral tribunal is not an organ of the State in which it has its seat in the same way that a court of the seat would be.
>
> The primary source of the Tribunal's powers is the parties' agreement to arbitrate. An important consequence of this is that the Tribunal has a duty vis-à-vis the parties to ensure that their arbitration agreement is not frustrated. In certain circumstances, it may be necessary to decline to comply with an order issued by a court of the seat, in the fulfilment of the Tribunal's larger duty to the parties.

Of course, this is not to say that a contract, including an arbitration agreement, has a validity that is independent of any legal order. Indeed, a contract derives its binding force from its recognition by one or more legal orders. However, an agreement to submit disputes to international arbitration is not anchored exclusively in the legal order of the seat of the arbitration. Such agreements are validated by a range of international sources and norms extending beyond the domestic seat itself" [37].

Perhaps even more telling of the Tribunal's courage and its view of the interaction between international arbitration and the legal order of the seat of the arbitration, was its further finding that:

"The Tribunal owes a duty to the parties to ensure that their agreement to submit disputes to international arbitration is rendered effective even where that creates a *conflict with the courts of the seat of the arbitration.*" [38]

Arbitration case law has developed a body of decisions whereby arbitrators have relied on the principle of competence-competence, which supports their power to rule on their own jurisdiction and determine the existence, validity and scope of the arbitration agreement; the same principle entails the arbitrators' power to give effect to the arbitration agreement and to enjoin parties from initiating or participating in court proceedings in breach of such an agreement.

For example, the Sole Arbitrator in ICC Case No. 8307 noted:

"[T]he agreement to arbitrate implies that the parties have renounced to submit to judicial courts the disputes envisaged by the arbitral clause. If a party despite this commences a judicial action when an arbitration is pending, it not only violates the rule according to which a dispute between the same parties over the same subject can be decided by one judge only, but also the binding arbitration clause . . . [A]n arbitrator has the power to order the parties to comply with their contractual commitments. The agreement to arbitrate being one of them, its violation must

37. *Salini Costruttori SpA* v. *The Federal Democratic Republic of Ethiopia, Addis Ababa Water and Sewerage Authority*, Award of 7 December 2001, ICC Case No. 10623, in *IAI Series on International Arbitration No. 2. Anti-Suit Injunctions in International Arbitration*, paras. 127-129.

38. *Ibid.*, para. 138 (emphasis added).

> be dealt with in the same manner when it is patent that the action initiated in a state court is outside the jurisdiction of such court and is therefore abusive." [39]

Likewise, in a *Gazprom* v. *Lithuania* arbitration, the Tribunal held that it had "the power to order specific performance if it finds that the Respondent has breached the arbitration clause", such breach being constituted, in the Tribunal's finding, by investigation proceedings started before the courts in Lithuania [40].

Certain scholars may object that a party's right to its home judge is an absolute (sometimes constitutional) right that must be preserved and that arbitral jurisdiction should, in all those instances, surrender to court jurisdiction. This is precisely the breaking point of the relationship between the two legal orders: if it is enough for a party resisting international arbitration to invoke its right to its "own" judge, when it has accepted in a contract that the judge of that contract will be the arbitrator, for the seized national court to immediately intervene to the prejudice of the arbitration process and the other party's right to see the dispute be resolved by the chosen justice mechanism (including as regards matters of jurisdiction), then this means that international arbitration and the arbitrators' adjudicatory power will never be respected. This is no longer a matter of conflict, it is one denial of international arbitration as a system of justice. This shows why a representation that accepts international arbitration as a distinct legal system results in more disciplined, more harmonious and more coordinated interactions between international arbitration and national legal systems, without either system being denied in its existence and effectiveness.

39. *[A]* v. *[B] [C]*, ICC Case No. 8307/FMS/KGA, Interim Award (14 May 2001), in *Anti-Suit Injunctions in International Arbitration*, Emmanuel Gaillard (ed.), 2005, p. 307, paras. 9-10, cited in E. Gaillard, "Coordination or Chaos: Do the Principles of Comity, *Lis Pendens*, and *Res Judicata* Apply to International Arbitration?", *op. cit.*, p. 217.

40. *OAO Gazprom* v. *Ministry of Energy of the Republic of Lithuania*, SCC Case No. V 125/2011, Final Award (31 July 2012), cited in E. Gaillard, "Coordination or Chaos: Do the Principles of Comity, *Lis Pendens*, and *Res Judicata* Apply to International Arbitration?", *op. cit.*, pp. 217-218.

CHAPTER III

POSSIBILITIES FOR INTER-SYSTEMIC COOPERATION BETWEEN THE ARBITRAL LEGAL ORDER AND NATIONAL LEGAL ORDERS

A final question is whether the concepts of coordination or conflict exhaust the question of the relationship between national and arbitral legal orders.

In the Course I had the honor of giving at this Academy in 2019 on the powers of the arbitrators, I proposed, on this subject, to recognize that the arbitral legal process may play fully its role as a system of justice through *judicial cooperation* with national legal orders.

The concept of cooperation is not new to international arbitration. Arbitration law is familiar with the possibility offered to the parties, in certain laws, to have recourse to the *"juge d'appui"*, namely the national court intervening in support of arbitration, for example in relation to the constitution of an arbitral tribunal. On this subject, and following the *NIOC* case law, the 2011 French law on arbitration has even allowed, in Article 1505 (4) of the Code of Civil Procedure, the French judge acting in support of arbitration to intervene when "one of the parties is exposed to a risk of a denial of justice"[41].

"Appui" or support means, indeed, that national courts, in these instances, are available to assist the arbitral process. Other examples exist, notably in evidentiary matters: resorting to the competent judge to assist with obtaining documentary or witness evidence that can then be used in arbitration. An example is to be found in Article 184 (2) of the Swiss Private International Law, which provides that "[i]f the assistance of the judicial or administrative authorities of the State is needed to take evidence, the arbitral tribunal or, with the consent of

41. "Article 1505

In international arbitration, and unless otherwise stipulated, the judge acting in support of the arbitration shall be the President of the Tribunal de grande instance of Paris when:

(1) the arbitration takes place in France; or
(2) the parties have agreed that French procedural law shall apply to the arbitration; or
(3) the parties have expressly granted jurisdiction to French courts over disputes relating to the arbitral procedure; or
(4) one of the parties is exposed to a risk of a denial of justice."

the arbitral tribunal, a party may request the assistance of the judge at the seat of the arbitral tribunal who shall apply his own law". Another example is provided by Article 42 of the English Arbitration Act, which provides that the "court may make an order requiring a party to comply with a peremptory order made by the tribunal", provided that the court "is satisfied that the applicant has exhausted any available arbitral process in respect of failure to comply with the tribunal's order"[42]. French law has adopted a slightly different approach, requiring that the party's request be authorized by the arbitrators:

> "If one of the parties to arbitral proceedings intends to rely on an official *(acte authentique)* or private *(acte sous seing privé)* deed to which it was not a party, or on *evidence held by a third party*, it may, *upon leave of the arbitral tribunal*, have that third party summoned before the President of the Tribunal de grande instance for the purpose of obtaining a copy thereof *(expédition)* or the production of the deed or item of evidence."[43]

Do these examples not illustrate instances of true cooperation between different adjudicators? In her inspired study on judicial cooperation, based on her doctoral dissertation, Professor Kamalia Mehtiyeva defines cooperation as follows:

> "a procedural document issued by the judge of the requesting legal order aimed at the requested legal order and asking the latter to deploy its means in order to contribute to the resolution of the dispute pending before the requesting judge. In responding to this

---

42. 1996 English Arbitration Act, Article 42:

"(1) Unless otherwise agreed by the parties, the court may make an order requiring a party to comply with a peremptory order made by the tribunal.

(2) An application for an order under this section may be made –

(a) by the tribunal (upon notice to the parties)
(b) by a party to the arbitral proceedings with the permission of the tribunal (and upon notice to the other parties), or
(c) where the parties have agreed that the powers of the court under this section shall be available.

(3) The court shall not act unless it is satisfied that the applicant has exhausted any available arbitral process in respect of failure to comply with the tribunal's order.

(4) No order shall be made under this section unless the court is satisfied that the person to whom the tribunal's order was directed has failed to comply with it within the time prescribed in the order or, if no time was prescribed, within a reasonable time."

43. French Code of Civil Procedure, Article 1469 (emphasis added).

request, the requested judge is not required to cooperate, but may do so either on the basis of an international agreement, or based on comity and a hope for reciprocity" [44].

Judicial cooperation is thus based on the request made by the judge of a requiring legal order to the judge of a requested legal order for purposes of a pending dispute before the former. What are arbitrators other than adjudicators whose function consists of administering justice? To borrow from Professor Charles Jarrosson, the concept of *"jurisdictio"* is "part of the imperium that entails the *power to state the law* [adjudicate], a power conferred by the State upon the judge and, subject to certain conditions, to the arbitrator" [45].

Viewed from the standpoint of administration of justice, there is today no bar to the full recognition of arbitrators – be they recognized as organs of the arbitral legal order or, for those resisting the concept, as the ordinary adjudicators of international disputes whose tasks and duties include the safeguarding of international public policy – as *subjects* of international cooperation with other judges, and no longer the mere *objects* of court intervention (be it in support of arbitration or, to the contrary, to disrupt the arbitral process).

There are practical consequences to the cooperation, and thus, the dialogue that can be engaged among courts and arbitrators. An example may be found, in the context of allegations of corruption, in the increasing number of interactions between arbitral and criminal proceedings. In the more traditional situations, the existence of criminal investigations or proceedings may result in certain types of evidence finding their way into arbitral proceedings, in support or in defense of a party's allegation of corruption. To the extent allegations of corruption concern a State party to the arbitration, as is the case in investment arbitration, nothing in principle prevents arbitrators from addressing their requests to the criminal prosecutors or courts of that State party, generally through orders given to the State itself. But one

44. K. Mehtiyeva, *La notion de coopération judiciaire*, LGDJ, 2020, para. 491 ("un acte de procédure pris par le juge de l'ordre juridique requérant destiné à un ordre juridique requis et demandant à ce dernier de mettre en œuvre ses moyens afin de contribuer à la résolution du litige pendant devant le juge requérant. En réponse à cette demande, le juge requis n'est pas contraint de coopérer, mais le fait soit en application d'une convention internationale, soit sur le fondement d'une simple courtoisie et un espoir de réciprocité").

45. Ch. Jarrosson, "Réflexions sur l'*imperium*", *Etudes offertes à Pierre Bellet*, Paris, Litec, 1991, pp. 245-279, para. 81 *in fine* ("une composante de l'imperium qui réside dans le *pouvoir de dire le droit*, pouvoir conféré par l'Etat au juge et, sous certaines conditions et limites, à l'arbitre") (emphasis added).

may go one step further, when the criminal court looking into a relevant matter is that of a third State: the concept of cooperation would allow the arbitrators to show a legitimate interest in obtaining evidence that is in the hands of such third State's courts or prosecutors. One step further yet: today, instances exist in which evidence that has surfaced *in arbitral proceedings* – through document production, for example – may give rise to the initiation of criminal investigations in the home State of one of the parties or, in more complex cases, even in third States. The question then, from a judicial cooperation standpoint, is whether arbitrators may be requested by the criminal prosecutors or courts of one State to provide the evidence that has been gathered in the arbitration and that may be of use in their criminal investigations or proceedings, and what their answer should be in these situations.

All these examples show that, from the judicial cooperation angle – which is designed to allow the requesting court to accomplish its own task of administration of justice in its own legal order – arbitrators have as much the ability to cooperate in the administration of justice by national courts in the latter's national legal orders, as national courts have the ability to cooperate in the administration of justice by the arbitrators in international arbitration (or the arbitral legal order for those who view arbitration as such). In this manner, each system is susceptible of making use of the other to achieve its own effectiveness.

* * *

Conflict and coordination, transcended perhaps by the concept of cooperation: ultimately, the interaction between national legal orders and the arbitral legal order (or, simply international arbitration) comes down to the perception we all have of the arbitrators' role and duties in the administration of international justice and the extent to which national legal systems (including courts) are willing to recognize a principal or a residual role to the arbitrators in fulfilling their task when parties have consented to resolve their dispute through arbitration.

Whether or not this interaction can, or must seek to, achieve harmony – which the proponents of the monolocal view of arbitration put forward as a key value [46] – is, in fact, not the question. In his Legal

46. E. Gaillard, *Legal Theory of International Arbitration, op. cit.*, para. 17: "The view that holds international arbitration as being exclusively anchored in the legal order of the country of the seat appears to find its main justification in a form of State positivism and in an *exacerbated quest for legal harmony*. In other words, international arbitration can only stem from States and, in order to avoid 'chaos', from one particular State." (emphasis added).

Theory of International Arbitration, Professor Gaillard noted that an international harmony of solutions is hardly achievable given the way in which international arbitration is currently structured and viewed:

> "An international harmony of solutions can, in reality, only come about if all States adopt identical arbitration legislation and, above all, if the adopted solutions are applied uniformly by the courts of each State. Despite the efforts made internationally towards such harmonization, one must admit, to be realistic, that arbitration laws and, more significantly, the attitude of the various national courts towards arbitration, differ considerably." [47]

In this context, I want to leave the last word to Professor Gaillard, from his Myth of Harmony in International Arbitration:

> "As Roscoe Pound lucidly noted more than a century ago, the law 'must be judged by the results it achieves, not by the niceties of its internal structure [or] by the beauty of its logical processes'. This observation is particularly relevant today, as lawyers and NGOs hostile to globalization often manipulate the notion of harmony in order to achieve certain results or promote certain ideologies in the field of international arbitration. In this construct, harmony is placed above justice, *in defavorem arbitrandum* and, paradoxically, its mechanical application produces inharmonious results. This can be avoided by understanding that achieving harmony in this mechanical way is not the best possible option for international arbitration and that the lack of a mechanical harmony should not be lamented, as a little bit of chaos, as in any other system, is necessary for its evolution." [48]

---

47. E. Gaillard, *Legal Theory of International Arbitration*, *op. cit.*, para. 22.
48. E. Gaillard, "The Myth of Harmony in International Arbitration", *op. cit.*, p. 568.

LES REPRÉSENTATIONS DE L'ARBITRAGE À TRAVERS LA JURISPRUDENCE

par

Dominique Hascher*

1. Dans son cours à l'Académie qu'il consacre aux «Aspects philosophiques du droit de l'arbitrage international», Gaillard nous enseigne que la représentation de l'arbitrage international est une construction mentale qui définit l'ensemble de la matière de l'arbitrage [1]. La représentation rend compte de l'approche de la matière dans sa globalité :

> «Seules les conceptions de nature à rendre compte de manière globale du phénomène arbitral, de ses sources, de ses fins et de ses structures retiendront à titre principal notre attention. Les représentations de l'arbitrage commercial international les plus structurantes nous paraissent être aujourd'hui au nombre de trois. La première réduit l'arbitrage international à une composante d'un ordre juridique donné, la seconde en trouve le fondement dans une pluralité d'ordres juridiques étatiques, et la troisième, qui est celle de l'auteur du présent cours, est celle de l'ordre juridique arbitral.» [2]

2. Trois conceptions émergent donc.

– La représentation monolocalisatrice, qui place l'arbitrage sous la responsabilité de la loi du siège :

> «… consiste à assimiler purement et simplement l'arbitre à une juridiction d'un ordre juridique unique, qui se trouve être l'ordre juridique du siège de l'arbitrage, le siège étant conçu comme un for. Dans cette conception, une sentence est moins internationale que colombienne ou anglaise, du seul fait que l'arbitrage s'est déroulé en Colombie ou en Angleterre, et la source de sa juridicité est trouvée exclusivement dans le droit de l'Etat dans lequel l'arbitrage a eu lieu» [3].

---

* Conseiller à la Cour de cassation de France.

1. *Aspects philosophiques du droit de l'arbitrage international*, Adi-Poche, Martinus Nijhoff Publishers, 2008 : «Ce sont ces représentations qui structurent la pensée juridique en la matière», par. 7.

2. *Ibid.*, par. 10.

3. *Ibid.*, par. 11.

– La deuxième représentation, multilocalisatrice, qu'il qualifie de modèle « "westphalien" par analogie avec l'ordre mondial de juxtaposition de puissances souveraines qui s'est établi pour la société internationale après la paix de Westphalie de 1648 » [4]:

> « [e]st celle qui trouve la juridicité de la sentence, non dans le seul ordre juridique du siège, mais dans l'ensemble des ordres juridiques prêts, à certaines conditions, à reconnaître l'efficacité de la sentence. Dans cette optique, multilocalisatrice tandis que la précédente était monolocalisatrice, le droit du siège de l'arbitrage, sans être éliminé complètement, n'est plus qu'un droit parmi d'autres. Il ne s'agit plus de la source exclusive du pouvoir de juger des arbitres. Tous les droits susceptibles d'entrer en contact avec l'arbitrage concerné ont une vocation égale à se prononcer sur la validité de la sentence, ceux des lieux éventuels d'exécution ayant un titre au moins aussi fort à le faire que celui du lieu de déroulement des opérations d'arbitrage … La sentence n'est plus comprise comme spécifiquement colombienne ou anglaise. Son caractère international l'emporte sur un rattachement exclusif au siège… » [5].

– La troisième représentation selon laquelle la juridicité de l'arbitrage ne résulte plus d'ordres juridiques étatiques spécifiques comme celui du siège avec la première représentation ou ceux d'exécution de la sentence avec la seconde représentation, considère :

> « que la juridicité de l'arbitrage puisse être puisée non dans un ordre juridique étatique, qu'il s'agisse de celui du siège ou de celui des lieux d'exécution, mais dans un ordre juridique tiers, susceptible d'être qualifié d'ordre juridique arbitral » [6].

Il n'est pas sans importance de remarquer que les trois visions proposées sont toutes positivistes étatiques. Elles se différencient profondément en ce que dans la première représentation, il s'agit de l'Etat du siège, dans la seconde représentation, de l'Etat(s) de l'exécution et dans la troisième représentation, des Etats dans leur ensemble.

3. Son cours n'est pas resté une construction intellectuelle. Ses enseignements ont trouvé un public attentif chez les juges de l'arbitrage. Ont-ils toujours bien lu le cours ? Peu importe. Si les représentations de

4. *Aspects philosophiques*, par. 32.
5. *Ibid.*, par. 23.
6. *Ibid.*, par. 40.

l'arbitrage donnent une réponse à l'intégralité de la matière, les juges font des emprunts pour trouver une solution, ils prennent ce qu'ils aiment, mais pas obligatoirement pour la justesse de la vision évoquée dans le raisonnement, bien que ceux qui sont familiers de l'arbitrage devraient avoir une représentation et la développer d'une manière cohérente. La notion de représentation s'apparente d'ailleurs pour Gaillard à un acte de foi et va bien au-delà de la résolution d'un litige, comme il l'expose dans la conclusion de son Cours :

> « En présence de trois conceptions de l'arbitrage international qui, toutes, ont vocation à expliquer l'entier phénomène, on pourrait être tenté de se demander suivant quels critères il y aurait lieu de les départager. Une telle question n'aurait en réalité aucun sens s'agissant de représentations, de visions de l'institution qui, en tant que telles, relèvent du domaine de la croyance, sinon de la foi, et non de celui de la vérité scientifique. On n'insistera jamais assez sur le fait que, dans ce registre, il ne saurait être question de vrai ou de faux, mais seulement de cohérent ou d'incohérent, d'efficace ou d'inefficace. L'utilité d'identifier chacune de ces représentations et d'en évaluer les conséquences pratiques est ailleurs. Elle réside dans le souci de comprendre en profondeur les courants qui traversent le droit de l'arbitrage, de mesurer leur audience et surtout–mais c'est peut-être déjà prendre parti–d'apprécier le sens de l'évolution. » [7]

4. Chaque représentation est cohérente, à suivre l'ensemble. De manière générale, plutôt que d'adopter une vision au départ dont va découler la solution de leur décision les juges légitiment de préférence une solution en cherchant un fondement doctrinal comme nous le glisse Gaillard en évoquant un acte de foi, la représentation est intuitive et implicite. Voici qui explique que la jurisprudence est traversée de courants souvent contraires, même si la poursuite d'une politique juridictionnelle cohérente doit être un objectif. Je m'intéresserai prioritairement aux décisions qui ont mentionné ses travaux dans leur raisonnement sur la convention d'arbitrage et la sentence. Sans prétendre à aucun caractère exhaustif, elles m'ont paru les plus incitatives à provoquer la réflexion.

---

7. *Aspects philosophiques*, par. 135.

CHAPITRE I

LA CONVENTION D'ARBITRAGE

A. Compétence-compétence et priorité à l'arbitrage

5. La doctrine de compétence-compétence est accueillie dans la plupart des législations actuelles sur l'arbitrage. Elle «fait aujourd'hui partie de ces règles qui paraissent unanimement admises mais qui, en réalité, dissimulent encore de profondes divergences en droit comparé»[8]. De fait, l'utilisation de cette règle est sujette à des conséquences très différentes selon la représentation de l'arbitrage à l'œuvre.

6. Dans la représentation monolocalisatrice, qui embrigade les juridictions arbitrales dans l'ordre juridique du siège comme toute autre juridiction de l'Etat, la compétence respective des juges et des arbitres est départagée par l'exception de litispendance. On en trouve une illustration dans l'arrêt *Fomento*[9] du Tribunal fédéral suisse obligeant l'arbitre qui siège en Suisse à surseoir à statuer dans l'attente de la décision de la juridiction étrangère susceptible d'y être reconnue.

7. Dans le modèle westphalien, le recours à l'exception de litispendance devient sans intérêt, souligne Gaillard, dans la mesure où, chaque ordre juridique se prononçant sur la validité et l'existence de la clause, la réponse apportée par les juridictions de chaque Etat est indifférente[10]. C'est désormais le point de vue du droit suisse.[11] La délimitation de la compétence du juge et de l'arbitre pour se prononcer sur la validité de la convention d'arbitrage devient le domaine d'application de la règle de compétence-compétence[12].

---

8. E. Gaillard, «L'effet négatif de la compétence-compétence», *Etudes Jean-François Poudret*, Lausanne, 1999, p. 387.

9. TF 14 mai 2001, *Fomento*, Rev. arb. 2001.835, note J.-F. Poudret.

10. *Aspects philosophiques*, par. 83.

11. Article 186, alinéa 1 *bis*, LDIP qui demande au tribunal arbitral de statuer sur sa compétence sans égard à une action ayant le même objet déjà pendante entre les mêmes parties devant une autre juridiction, *Aspects philosophiques*, par. 85. E. Gaillard, «La reconnaissance, en droit suisse, de la seconde moitié du principe d'effet négatif de la compétence-compétence», dans *Global Reflections on International Law, Commerce and Dispute Resolution, Liber Amicorum in Honour of Robert Briner*, ICC Publication n° 693, 2005, p. 311.

12. J.-P. Ancel, «La Cour de cassation et les principes fondateurs de l'arbitrage international», dans *Mélanges Pierre Drai, Dalloz*, 2000, p. 161.

8. La répartition de compétences est une question de coordination entre les ordres juridiques étatiques et l'ordre juridique arbitral. Dans cette dernière représentation, Gaillard nous montre que la compétence arbitrale ne se réduit pas à identifier l'arbitre à une juridiction comme une autre parmi toutes celles qui pourraient être saisies du litige :

> « c'est en vertu d'un mécanisme propre à cet ordre juridique, et non par emprunt à l'idée de litispendance, destinée à départager des juridictions ayant une égale vocation à trancher un même litige, que le conflit entre une juridiction arbitrale et une juridiction étatique doit être réglé. Ce mécanisme réside dans le principe de compétence-compétence. Celui-ci donne à l'arbitre dont la compétence est contestée le pouvoir de trancher lui-même les questions dont dépend sa compétence, sans que l'on puisse lui opposer l'argument selon lequel il ne pourrait le faire sans illogisme puisqu'on ne sait pas encore, à ce stade, s'il sera ou non compétent » [13].

9. L'un des apports majeurs de la doctrine de Gaillard est d'avoir dégagé de l'effet positif de la règle de compétence-compétence, qui s'adresse à l'arbitre, celle qu'il a appelée l'effet négatif, qui s'adresse au juge en lui interdisant de se prononcer sur la validité de la clause d'arbitrage tant que l'arbitre n'a rien décidé. Concrètement, l'effet négatif de la règle de compétence-compétence s'exprime sous la forme d'une règle de priorité à l'arbitrage selon laquelle le juge étatique attend l'arbitre. Nombreux sont aujourd'hui les droits de l'arbitrage qui acceptent la règle [14]. L'influence de Gaillard est ici palpable et a été mise en valeur, en Asie notamment, entre autres dans le droit chinois, ou dans les droits latino-américains ou encore récemment à Maurice [15].

---

13. *Aspects philosophiques*, par. 83, p. 128.

14. E. Gaillard, « Dialogue des ordres juridiques : ordre juridique arbitral et ordres juridiques étatiques », *Rev. arb.* 2018.493. E. Gaillard et Y. Banifatemi, « Negative Effect of Competence-Competence : The Rule of Priority in Favour of the Arbitrators », dans *Enforcement of Arbitration Agreements and International Arbitral Awards*, Cameron Mai 2008, p. 257.

15. P. Fu et X. Herrera-Bernal, « Le rayonnement de la pensée d'Emmanuel Gaillard en droit de l'arbitrage commercial international », dans *Hommage à Emmanuel Gaillard : une pensée en action, JDI* 2022.1203. P. Fu, « The Doctrine of Kompetenz-Kompetenz : A Sino-French Comparative Perspective » (2022) HKLJ, vol. 52, part. 3, p. 1. A. Reyes, *The Practice of International Commercial Arbitration, A Handbook for Hong Kong Arbitrators*, Informa Law from Routledge, 2018. *Alliance Building* v. *Seafarers* (2023) SCJ 128.

10. Parmi les juridictions qui se sont exprimées en faveur de la règle de priorité, c'est à Singapour que l'on a été le plus disert [16]. L'adoption de la règle a été consacrée dans les termes qui suivent :

> «. . . First, the *prima facie* approach coheres better with what we consider was envisaged by the drafters of the IAA [International arbitration Act. . .].
>
> Second, to require the court, on a stay application under s. 6 of the IAA, to undertake a full determination of an arbitral tribunal's jurisdiction could significantly hollow the *kompetenz-kompetenz* principle of its practical effect. The full merits approach has the potential to reduce an arbitral tribunal's *kompetenz-kompetenz* to a contingency dependent on the strategic choices of the claimant in a putative arbitration. If the claimant decides to pursue its claim by arbitration, the arbitral tribunal will determine any challenge to its jurisdiction, and thus, its *kompetenz-kompetenz* will be given full vent. But, if the claimant decides to pursue its claim by bringing proceedings in court (*instead* of by recourse to arbitration), the court will be seized of jurisdiction, and will be able (and, indeed, on the full merits approach, obliged) to make a full determination on the existence and scope of the arbitration clause ; this will deprive the putative arbitral tribunal of its *kompetenz-kompetenz*. In our view, the strength of the *kompetenz-kompetenz* principle cannot depend on the arbitrary choice of the claimant as to whether it will pursue its claim by way of court proceedings or by way of arbitration. That undermines the principles of judicial non-intervention and *kompetenz-kompetenz* which were at the forefront in the drafting of the Model Law and the enactment of the original IAA. . .
>
> Third, we consider that the fear of resource duplication which, it is said, will arise from the *prima facie* approach is overstated.

---

16. En commençant avec The «Titan Unity» [2013] SGHCR 28 :

«. . . the court's role at the early stage to determine on a prima facie standard whether there exists an arbitration agreement between the parties in deciding whether a stay can be granted under section 6 of the IAA [International Arbitration Act], is consistent with the approach of having a full determination of that question deferred to the arbitral tribunal subject to ultimate court control at the end of the whole arbitral life cycle, with the control taking the form of either the setting aside of the award via Article 34 (2) *(a) (i)* of the Model Law or the refusal of enforcement via Article V (1) *(a)* of the New York Convention, both of which have the force of law in Singapore, and which confer upon the court the full jurisdiction to review and determine on the merits whether there exists an arbitration agreement concluded between the parties. . .» (par. 29).

A robust recognition and enforcement of the *kompetenz-kompetenz* principle may, on the contrary, deter a plaintiff from commencing proceedings in court in the face of an arbitration agreement. The plaintiff will be well aware that the court will stay the proceedings in favour of arbitration except in cases where the arbitration clause is *clearly* invalid or inapplicable. . . » [17]

11. Cette jurisprudence nous apprend beaucoup sur son point d'ancrage parmi les représentations de l'arbitrage. Là où Gaillard avait souligné que la jurisprudence Fomento consistait à assimiler l'arbitre siégeant en Suisse au juge suisse [18], la jurisprudence de Singapour prend résolument le parti d'une application de la règle de priorité, où que soit le siège de l'arbitrage :

> « I add here parenthetically that there appears to be some suggestion from the materials submitted that there could be a hybrid approach taken, such that a prima facie standard of review be adopted when the seat of the arbitration is in the jurisdiction of the court seized of the stay application, while a full determination on the existence of an arbitration agreement be made where the seat of arbitration is located in a foreign jurisdiction [referring to some decisions of the Swiss courts] It was not submitted by counsel that this hybrid approach should be the approach in Singapore. This court is any event not in favour of such an approach, which appears to be tainted by circularity. The seat of arbitration may not be known until arbitral proceedings have commenced, and it would not be uncommon where arbitration proceedings are not commenced until the stay of court proceedings has been granted in the first place. The approach also fails to acknowledge the fact that the seat of an arbitration may be transferred amidst arbitral proceedings. » [19]

12. La solution est cohérente avec les représentations de l'arbitrage qui refusent la litispendance pour départager juge et arbitre. On peut ainsi noter une décision de la cour d'appel de Paris allant dans le même sens [20]. Faire dépendre, comme l'a proposé la jurisprudence

---

17. *Tomolugen Holdings Ltd.* v. *Silica Investors Ltd.* (2015) SGCA 57, par. 65, 67-68.

18. E. Gaillard, « Souveraineté et autonomie : réflexions sur les représentations de l'arbitrage international », *JDI*, 2007.1163, n° 16.

19. The « Titan Unity » (2013) SGHCR 28, par. 30.

20. CA Paris, 4 décembre 2002, *Rev. arb.* 2003.1286, note E. Gaillard.

suisse, l'application de la règle de priorité selon que l'arbitrage se tient dans l'Etat du for ou à l'étranger, est un critère bien ténu, comme le remarquait Gaillard [21], pour conditionner l'étendue de l'examen de l'exception d'arbitrage, ce que le juge de Singapour avait noté en évoquant une approche circulaire quand le siège est inconnu avant le début de la procédure arbitrale ou est modifié en cours de procédure.

13. La règle de priorité a l'avantage d'éviter les inconciliabilités de décisions en ramenant la compétence à deux examens successifs, par l'arbitre, puis, le cas échéant, par le juge. Adoptant les propositions de Gaillard, les juridictions de Singapour s'y réfèrent comme un avantage de la règle qui permet de rationaliser le contentieux judiciaire en le concentrant sur le contrôle de la sentence :

> «... the position emanates from the judicial policy of consolidating the court's review of international arbitration disputes at the end of the arbitral life cycle, so that the court's fullest jurisdiction to determine the validity of an arbitration agreement remain with the same courts having jurisdiction to conduct a full review of an arbitral award under the limited grounds provided in Article V of the New York Convention (Emmanuel Gaillard and Yas Banifatemi, Negative effect of Competence-Competence : the Rule of Priority in Favour of the arbitrators, in Enforcement of Arbitration Agreements and International Arbitral Awards : The New York Convention in Practice 257-258, Gaillard and Di Pietro (eds.), 2008)) [22]».

14. Le positionnement du juge et de l'arbitre varie selon la représentation de référence. Bien que dans la deuxième représentation comme dans la troisième, le juge ne sera appelé à statuer qu'en cas de contestation de la compétence arbitrale lors du contrôle de la sentence, on est davantage dans un modèle westphalien lorsque le juge, tout en appliquant la règle de priorité, sursoit simplement à statuer dans l'attente de la décision de l'arbitre [23].

21. E. Gaillard, «La reconnaissance en droit suisse de la seconde moitié du principe d'effet négatif de la compétence-compétence», *Liber Amicorum Robert Briner*, ICC, 2005, p. 311.

22. *First Link Investments Corp Ltd.* v. *GT Payment Pte Ltd.* (2014) SGHCR 12, par. 7 *(c)*. Voir aussi, The «Titan Unity» [2013] SGHCR 28, par. 29.

23. *Tomolugen Holdings Ltd.* v. *Silica Investors Ltd.* [2015] SGCA 57 :

> «We therefore hold that in considering a stay application under s 6 of the IAA, the court need only be satisfied to a *prima facie* standard that the requirements for the grant of a stay under that section have been met before ordering a stay. Our subsequent discussion of the issues in these appeals should therefore be construed

15. La représentation fondée sur l'ordre juridique arbitral tire une conséquence plus drastique. Dans cette vision, la compétence du juge étatique n'est plus suspendue le temps de l'arbitrage, pour éventuellement reprendre, comme si la justice étatique était la règle et l'arbitrage l'exception [24]. Le juge étatique n'étant, par hypothèse, pas le juge de la contestation dont le règlement se situe dans un ordre juridique tiers par rapport aux ordres juridiques étatiques, un sursis à statuer manquerait de sens dans une telle représentation, même si le juge sera éventuellement amené à se prononcer sur la décision de l'arbitre sur sa compétence en cas de recours. Aussi, le juge se déclare simplement incompétent comme on le voit dans la jurisprudence française qui adhère à la représentation de l'ordre juridique arbitral.

16. Il est dans la logique de la règle de priorité que tous les arguments, développés ou non devant l'arbitre pour soutenir ou combattre la compétence arbitrale, puissent être débattus lors du contrôle de la décision sur la compétence, au moment où le juge étatique examine pour la première fois la question. Cette proposition est d'autant plus forte dans la représentation de l'ordre juridique arbitral que le départage avec l'ordre juridique étatique est une question de pouvoir juridictionnel dont la résolution ne doit pas être abandonnée à une poignée d'arguments seulement [25].

17. La cohérence entre la priorité donnée à l'arbitre et le principe de validité de la convention d'arbitrage a été mise en valeur par la jurisprudence française [26]. Donnant à l'autonomie de la clause d'arbitrage une dimension supplémentaire à celle de séparabilité du contrat dans laquelle elle est généralement entendue, ce principe émancipe la clause d'arbitrage de tout droit étatique déterminé qui prétendrait la soumettre [27]. Substituer la volonté des parties au droit étatique pour s'assurer de l'existence et la validité de la clause d'arbitrage, comme le fait la jurisprudence *Dalico* [28], relève de la méthode des règles transnationales caractéristiques de l'ordre juridique arbitral, présentée par Gaillard comme permettant « de dégager aussi bien des règles

in this light by any arbitral tribunal that might in due course hear the dispute in the Suit. » (par. 70).

24. Convention de Genève de 1961, article VI (3).

25. Cass. civ. 1re, 2 décembre 2020, *Schooner*, nº 1915396.

26. Cass. civ. 1re, 7 juin 2006, *ABS*, nº 0312034 et Cass. civ. 1re, 5 janvier 1999, *Zanzi*, nº 9621430.

27. J.-P. Ancel, « La Cour de cassation et les principes fondateurs de l'arbitrage international », dans *Mélanges Pierre Drai*, Dalloz, 2000, p. 161.

28. Cass. civ. 1re, 20 décembre 1993, *Dalico*, nº 9116828.

supplétives que des règles impératives au sens du droit interne et des règles d'ordre public réellement international, correspondant en droit international, au *jus cogens* »[29]. Si Gaillard ne prône pas dans son cours un ordre juridique arbitral fondé sur la volonté des parties mais sur les ordres juridiques étatiques travaillant de manière collective, il faut lire Dalico dans le contexte d'une reconnaissance quasi universelle dans les systèmes de droit contemporains de la volonté des parties créatrice de droits.

B. La recherche du droit applicable à la convention d'arbitrage

18. Vous trouvez dans la jurisprudence française l'une des traductions possibles de la représentation de l'ordre juridique arbitral dans le droit positif. Il faut reconnaître que la représentation monolocalisatrice exprimée dans son état pur par les résolutions de l'Institut de droit international de 1952 et 1957[30] ne trouve plus beaucoup d'expression dans le droit contemporain. Une éclatante représentation westphalienne est illustrée par la règle de conflit de l'article 178 LDIP qui aboutit, en multipliant des facteurs de rattachement alternatifs allant du droit choisi par les parties, à celui régissant l'objet du litige, notamment le droit applicable au contrat principal, ou enfin au droit suisse, à valider la clause d'arbitrage dans la quasi-totalité des cas, à l'instar de ce que ferait le principe de validité de la clause dans la jurisprudence française[31].

19. On s'éloigne toujours de la vision monolocalisatrice qui privilégie le rattachement à l'ordre juridique du siège[32], quand la convention d'arbitrage peut être régie par des règles de droit différentes de celles d'une loi étatique. La jurisprudence de Singapour donne à la loi suédoise du siège dans l'affaire *First Link Investments* une conséquence qui place la convention d'arbitrage dans la sphère des règles transnationales, règles qui, d'après Gaillard, peuvent être considérées comme propres à l'ordre juridique arbitral[33] :

---

29. *Aspects philosophiques176*, par. 61, p. 86.

30. Annuaire de l'Institut de droit international, session d'Amsterdam, 1957, vol. 47, tome II, p. 479 (art. 5 : « la validité de la clause compromissoire est régie par la loi du siège du tribunal arbitral »).

31. E. Gaillard et P. Lalive, « Le nouveau droit de l'arbitrage international en Suisse », *JDI* 1989.905.

32. *Op. cit.*, par. 18.

33. *Op. cit.*, par. 60 : « la représentation selon laquelle l'arbitrage international s'organise en un régime présentant tous les attributs d'un véritable ordre juridique se manifeste essentiellement par l'utilisation de la méthode des règles transnationales par les arbitres ».

«. . . Assuming *arguendo* if the arbitration agreement is governed by the "laws" of the SCC [Stockholm Chamber of Commerce] as opposed to any national law, this does not necessarily demand a conclusion that the agreement is invalid and consequently unenforceable for the purposes of a stay application . . . It follows that, in so far as parties' intentions are to be given effect to, the reference to "law" need not necessarily be read as "law" in the conventional Hartian, Dworkinian or Razian sense. At least in the realm of international arbitration, it is not entirely inconceivable that a dispute over the validity of an arbitration agreement may be resolved by rules of law as opposed to national laws. . .

Yet the true difficulty is not that no law exists in which to answer these questions [if an arbitration agreement is void for lack of capacity or lack of consent] – there exists such a law – this would, according to Dalico, be the body of substantive international law on the formation of international arbitration agreements; the real issue here is that there is as yet no recognised body of international substantive rules which can provide the certainty the commercial world requires to determine the validity of an international arbitration agreement . . . This however does not mean that such a recognised body of international substantive rules applicable to international arbitration will never been formed. For a start, there is much to be said of the fact that countries of different legal traditions have agreed upon a common international standard of determining the substantive validity of arbitration agreements as not being "null, inoperative or incapable of being performed" under Art. II (3) of the New York Convention, which may be considered a self-executing provision which prescribes substantive rules of international law to the formation and validity of international agreements . . . In this regard, a court seized of an application to enforce an international arbitration agreement should, when determining its validity, defer parochial notions to internationally harmonious and uniform conceptions of validity, so as to give effect to the internationalized form of dispute resolution process selected by parties. . .

In so far as an international arbitration agreement may in theory be governed by a substantive body of international law instead of a national law, and to the extent where the rules and principles of an international arbitral institution reflect the legal principles and best practices found in this body of international law, a good argument can be made that there should be no conceptual limit on parties' autonomy in the present case to decide that the validity of their arbitration agreement should be determined by a clear system of rules and body of principles of the SCC. . .

In view that it has already been decided above that the proper law of the arbitration agreement is the law of Sweden, there is no need to determine the question of whether an arbitration agreement governed by the "laws" of the SCC can be enforced, suffice to say that there does appear to be a clear system of rules and consistent application principles of the SCC which would guide arbitrants in determining the validity of an arbitration agreement, and which may persuade a court to find that, at least on the prima facie threshold, such an arbitration agreement would be valid, but only for the specific purpose of staying court proceedings, which does not preclude a full jurisdictional challenge before the arbitral tribunal, or a complete review of the question by the enforcement court. » [34]

20. Certes, le raisonnement est d'une grande complexité sur une problématique multiple qui mêle des interrogations sur la juridicité des règles transnationales en raison de leur éventuelle incomplétude [35] et paraît limiter de telles règles à une sous-catégorie des règles d'arbitrage de la Chambre de commerce de Stockholm. L'effort de ce juge pour reconnaître l'application de règles transnationales à la convention d'arbitrage doit néanmoins être souligné [36].

21. Statuant sur l'exequatur d'une sentence rendue en France dans l'affaire *Dallah*, la Cour suprême du Royaume-Uni soumet à la règle matérielle posée par la jurisprudence Dalico l'extension au gouvernement pakistanais de la convention d'arbitrage régie par le droit français [37] :

« [Dalico] suggests that arbitration agreements derive their existence, validity and effect from supra-national law, without it being necessary to refer to any national law. If so, that would not avoid the need to have regard to French law as "the law of

34. *First Link Investments Corp Ltd.* v. *GT Payment Pte Ltd.* [2014] SGHCR 12, par. 18-21.

35. M. Mustill, *The New Lex Mercatoria : The First Twenty-Five Years, Etudes Wilberforce*, Oxford, 1987, p. 149.

36. E. Gaillard, « Les vertus des règles matérielles appliquées à la convention d'arbitrage », *Rev. arb.* 2020.701.

37. Cass. civ. 1re, 20 décembre 1993, *Dalico*, no 9116828.

the country where the award was made" under Article V (1) *(a)* of the Convention and s.103 (2) *(b)* of the 1996 Act. The Cour de Cassation is, however, a national court, giving a French legal view of international arbitration; and Dallah and the Government agree that the true analysis is that French law recognises transnational principles as potentially applicable to determine the existence, validity and effectiveness of an international arbitration agreement, such principles being part of French law"...

In the light of the common ground between the parties, it is also unnecessary to engage with the competing representations of international arbitration lucidly discussed in Gaillard's Legal Theory of International Arbitration (2010), pp. 13-66. Whatever the juridical underpinning or autonomy of their role from the viewpoint of international arbitrators, the present case involves an application to enforce in the forum of a national court, subject to principles defined by s.103 of the 1996 Act and Article V of the New York Convention, upon the effect of which there is substantial, though not complete, agreement between the parties now before the Supreme Court. » [38]

22. Nous sommes face à un conflit de représentations. D'un côté, une règle de conflit préconisant un rattachement à la loi du siège menant à la désignation d'un droit national, en l'occurrence le droit français, lequel, de l'autre côté, se propose de résoudre les questions de la convention d'arbitrage par des règles matérielles, certes françaises par l'origine nationale de leurs prescripteurs, les juridictions françaises, mais qui ont l'ambition de reproduire les solutions résultant des règles transnationales de l'ordre juridique arbitral. En appliquant les règles matérielles qui forment le droit français de l'arbitrage international, la Cour suprême britannique se livre à un exercice de droit comparé, s'efforçant de statuer comme le juge français l'aurait fait [39]. L'autre manière de procéder aurait été, à l'instar de ce que font les juges français, d'appliquer directement des règles matérielles transposées de l'ordre juridique arbitral, au contenu on peut le supposer fortement identique à celui dégagé par le juge français. Dans cette hypothèse,

38. *Dallah Real Estate* v. *The Ministry of Religious Affairs, Government of Pakistan*, jugement du 3 novembre 2010 (2010) UKSC 46, par. 15, 16.

39. E. Gaillard, «Comparative Law in International Commercial Arbitration», dans *Le recours à la méthodologie du droit comparé en arbitrage international, Ius Comparatum*, AIDC, vol. 1, 2020, p. 1.

le juge anglais aurait alors appliqué des règles matérielles anglaises. Mais cela aurait été changer de représentation et, comme l'énonce encore une décision de Singapour à propos de la jurisprudence *Dalico*, « [s]uch a principle surely cannot escape from the fact that this remains ultimately an application of French private international law, which in and of itself provides no normative impetus for other countries to adopt » [40]. On trouve une nouvelle illustration de ce qu'un juge donné (ici le juge anglais) a lui-même une représentation de l'arbitrage et l'applique de manière spontanée, sans choix doctrinal.

23. La haute juridiction britannique entreprend un examen fouillé des relations entre les parties, à la recherche de leur intention commune de lier le gouvernement pakistanais [41], à l'existence de laquelle elle conclut négativement [42]. Saisie du recours en annulation, la cour d'appel de Paris juge l'inverse [43]. Une situation factuelle tendue peut expliquer que l'affaire *Dallah* se situait à la limite de ce qui pouvait être accepté pour étendre la clause compromissoire au gouvernement du Pakistan, ce que le tribunal arbitral lui-même avait reconnu. On se sépare ainsi entre juges britanniques et français sur le rôle du secrétaire du ministère des Affaires religieuses qui était en même temps celui du Trust, co-contractant de Dallah.

24. Une autre explication tient à la difficulté d'appliquer le droit étranger comme le ferait le juge étranger. S'efforçant de donner une application fidèle de la jurisprudence *Dalico*, la Cour suprême retient, comme test pour l'extension de la clause, la commune volonté de Dallah et du gouvernement du Pakistan. Le tableau qu'elle dresse des intentions du ministère pakistanais des Affaires religieuses au travers des actions de son secrétaire et des conséquences sur les intentions de Dallah est admirable de précision : « the search for a subjective common intention under the principle recognised by the French courts must be undertaken by examining, and so through the prism of, the parties'

40. *First Link Investments Corp Ltd.* v. *GT Payment Pte Ltd.* (2014) SGHCR 12, par. 19.

41. *Dallah Real Estate* v. *The Ministry of Religious Affairs, Government of Pakistan*, jugement du 3 novembre 2010 (2010) UKSC 46, par. 41- 66.

42. « The third re-examination by this court, in the light of the whole history, of the issue whether the Government was party to the Agreement, and so to its arbitration clause, leads to no different answer to that reached in the courts below. The arbitral tribunal's contrary reasoning is neither conclusive nor on examination persuasive in a contrary sense. As to the law, it is far from clear that the tribunal was directing its mind to common intention and, if it was, it approached the issue of common intention in terms differing significantly from those which a French court would adopt » (par. 66).

43. CA Paris, 17 février 2011, *Rev. arb.* 2012.369, note F.-X. Train.

conduct »[44]. Cette minutie rend-elle pour autant compte de l'application des règles matérielles que le droit français met en œuvre pour régler les questions concernant la convention d'arbitrage? La leçon d'anatomie de Rembrandt que vous pourrez admirer au Mauritshuis nous présente le corps du condamné avec beaucoup de réalisme. Mais cela ne suffit pas pour insuffler la vie.

25. En matière d'extension de la convention d'arbitrage à des non-signataires, le droit français pose une double présomption, celle d'une connaissance de la clause d'arbitrage induite des faits, et celle d'une volonté de l'accepter. La référence à la volonté s'explique par le respect du fondement contractuel de l'arbitrage, mais elle n'a en réalité qu'un rôle cosmétique, car elle est induite quasi automatiquement des faits objectifs de la situation. On peut expliquer ce mouvement d'objectivation par le souci d'éviter de donner à la volonté tacite des parties une interprétation arbitraire. Mais si on le rapporte à l'ensemble des situations impliquant des parties non signataires du contrat dans lequel la clause d'arbitrage est stipulée, parce qu'il y a eu notamment cession ou transmission du contrat d'origine, on observe que le fondement subjectif s'étiole à chaque cas d'application[45]. L'objectivation de la volonté traduit donc plus qu'une réaction aux incertitudes de la recherche de la volonté. La recherche subjective de l'intention des parties qui caractérise les règles d'interprétation en droit français, en comparaison de l'approche objective du droit anglais[46], rend compte des regrets du juge suprême du Royaume-Uni que le tribunal arbitral ait fait l'économie des intentions de Dallah[47]. Dans un environnement où la clause d'arbitrage est soumise à des règles matérielles, les règles d'interprétation du Code civil manquent de pertinence. Pour répondre à l'interrogation de la Cour suprême d'une manière cohérente avec la jurisprudence *Dalico*, il suffit de dire qu'à partir du moment où une partie comme Dallah sollicite l'application de la clause, elle est d'accord pour l'arbitrage, sa volonté se dégage. En droit français, on se base sur une série d'indices pour déduire la volonté d'étendre la

---

44. *Dallah Real Estate* v. *The Ministry of Religious Affairs, Government of Pakistan*, jugement du 3 novembre 2010 (2010) UKSC 46, par. 65.

45. I. Fadlallah et D. Hascher, *Les grandes décisions du droit de l'arbitrage commercial*, Dalloz, 2019, comm. n° 18. A. Rau, *The Allocation of Power between Arbitral Tribunals and State Courts*, Adi-Poche, Martinus Nijhoff Publishers, 2018.

46. H. Beale, B. Fauvarque-Cosson, J. Rutgers, D. Tallon et S. Vogenauer, *Contract Law*, Hart Publishing, 2010.

47. *Dallah Real Estate* v. *The Ministry of Religious Affairs, Government of Pakistan*, jugement du 3 novembre 2010 (2010) UKSC 46, par. 60, 63.

clause d'arbitrage. L'orfèvrerie judiciaire réalisée par les meilleurs juges de l'Angleterre contraste avec le caractère plus frustre et terne, en comparaison, de l'arrêt français. Mais la décision française traduit, au fond, le recul de la commune volonté des parties mise en exergue dans la jurisprudence *Dalico*. Au-delà de la prévisibilité des solutions, ce recul exprime une représentation selon laquelle l'arbitrage est le mode juridictionnel de droit commun des relations internationales et non une juridiction d'exception auxquelles les parties accèdent en renonçant à la compétence étatique de droit commun. Cette représentation est celle de l'ordre juridique arbitral dont l'arbitre est l'organe juridictionnel [48]. Les représentations de l'arbitrage sont donc utiles. La déclaration citée plus haut de la Cour suprême de ne plus y penser dans la mesure où les parties s'accordaient sur l'application des règles matérielles françaises a éloigné son raisonnement de l'essentiel tenant à la compréhension de celles-ci dans le contexte de la représentation de l'ordre juridique arbitral acceptée par le droit français. Cela n'aurait peut-être pas conduit à l'harmonie des solutions entre les juridictions concernées par la validité de la sentence, mais aurait pu contribuer à y mener.

26. Ultérieurement, dans l'affaire *Kout Food*, les mêmes juridictions vont à nouveau réserver un sort différent à une sentence rendue à Paris. Cette fois, les juges anglais vont décider que la convention d'arbitrage est régie par le droit anglais, soit la conclusion inverse des juges français qui la soumettent à la règle matérielle de la jurisprudence *Dalico* [49]. Le plus remarquable dans ces décisions est la conception opposée que l'on se fait, en droit anglais et français, du rôle des principes généraux du droit dont les arbitres devaient faire application aux termes de la convention d'arbitrage. Gaillard observe dans *Kout Food* que

> « la prédisposition de chaque juge à donner effet à une référence aux principes généraux du droit constitue manifestement une autre différence marquante dans la comparaison des deux systèmes juridiques » [50].

48. *Aspects philosophiques*, par. 60.
49. (2021) UKSC 48 ; CA Paris, 23 juin 2020, *Rev. arb.* 2020.839.
50. E. Gaillard, « Les vertus de la méthode des règles matérielles appliquées à la convention d'arbitrage », *Rev. arb.* 2020.701.

CHAPITRE II

LA SENTENCE

A. La résistance du siège

27. L'un des juges de la Cour suprême du Royaume-Uni qui ont rédigé l'arrêt dans l'affaire *Dallah*, Lord Mance, a synthétisé ce que l'on peut attendre de la représentation monolocalisatrice. Il s'agit pour l'essentiel de localiser un siège juridique (même s'il ne coïncide pas avec les opérations géographiques d'arbitrage) où la sentence est réputée rendue au sens de la Convention de New York et où une intervention judiciaire limitée peut avoir lieu pour assurer l'efficience de l'arbitrage, déterminer l'existence d'un accord d'arbitrage, remplacer les arbitres, prendre une *anti-suit injunction*, ordonner des mesures provisoires et contrôler la sentence [51].

28. Quand Gaillard oppose l'Etat du siège «qui accueille un arbitrage dans ses hôtels et ses centres de conférence» à l'Etat «qui permet la saisie et la vente d'actifs situés sur son territoire», il ne remet pas en cause la constatation de Lord Mance selon laquelle le choix du siège de l'arbitrage est loin d'être fortuit, car guidé notamment par des considérations de neutralité et d'impartialité [52]. Il avance qu'un Etat a un moindre intérêt de contrôler la sentence rendue sur son territoire dès lors que l'exécution de celle-ci n'y est pas réclamée [53]. Allant dans son sens, on peut remarquer qu'un nombre croissant de législations admettent la possibilité de renoncer au recours en annulation [54].

29. Dans la représentation monolocalisatrice, l'arbitrage est, comme toute activité, régi par la loi du siège; or,

> «[c]ontrairement à ce que pourrait laisser penser la présentation caricaturale qui en est parfois donnée, la conception qui fonde la juridicité de l'arbitrage sur une pluralité d'ordres juridiques ne considère pas que la convention d'arbitrage, les opérations d'arbitrage et la sentence qui en résulte reposent sur la seule

---

51. 30th Freshfields Arbitration Lecture, 4 novembre 2015.
52. *Ibid.*
53. *Aspects philosophiques*, par. 36.
54. Art. 192 LDIP, article 1717 alinéa 4 code judiciaire belge, article 51 loi suédoise sur l'arbitrage, article 1522 alinéa 1 CPC.

volonté des parties. Dans cette conception, la sentence n'est pas flottante» [55].

La représentation westphalienne et la représentation territorialiste, poursuit Gaillard,

> «s'opposent du point de vue de la méthode, en ce qu'elles appréhendent le même phénomène tantôt par son point de départ, tantôt par son point d'arrivée … C'est la reconnaissance de cette sentence qui valide rétrospectivement le processus. Cette inversion, qui s'analyse en une véritable révolution copernicienne, commande tout le raisonnement» [56].

30. Qu'en est-il lorsque le pouvoir des arbitres trouve sa source, non dans certains droits étatiques comme avec les deux premières représentations, mais dans l'ordre juridique arbitral fondé sur la collectivité normative des Etats ? La représentation de l'ordre juridique arbitral n'a pas été sans difficultés pour les juges auxquels il était demandé de contrôler la sentence. L'affaire *Prometheus Marine* procure un intéressant exemple d'une utilisation à rebours de cette représentation pour mettre en échec un arbitrage. L'arbitre n'ayant pas déterminé si l'arbitrage à Singapour était soumis à la loi de l'arbitrage interne ou international du siège, la recourante soutenait qu'il fallait considérer l'arbitrage comme délocalisé, ce qui, rendant la sentence impossible à exécuter, l'aurait condamnée au regard de l'ordre public. Se refusant à déduire du silence de l'arbitre une quelconque soumission de l'arbitrage à un système juridique transnational, la Cour suprême de Singapour relève :

> «In this regard, Singapore law, unlike say French law (see, for instance, the French Supreme Court's decision in Société PT Putrabali Adyamulia v Société Rena Holding et Société Mnugotia Est Epices [2007] Rev Arb 507 (at 514) enforcing an arbitral award set aside by the English High Court, which was perceived as a judicial manifestation of the delocalisation theory), does not support the notion that arbitral proceedings or arbitral awards can stand free from control of the national legal system of the seat of the arbitration.» [57]

55. *Aspects philosophiques*, par. 27 en écho à l'arrêt anglais *Bank Mellat* v. *Hellinki Teckniki* ((1984) 1 QB 291) : «our jurisprudence does not recognize the concept of arbitral procedures floating in the transnational firmament, unconnected with any municipal system of law».

56. *Op. cit.*, par. 24.

57. *Prometheus Marine Pte* v. *King, Ann Rita and another* (2017) SGCA 61, par. 46.

31. Dire qu'une sentence n'est pas une sentence nationale au regard de la procédure applicable et des intérêts en jeu est une chose; dire, comme l'a fait le juge français dans l'affaire *Götaverken* [58], que le juge du siège, ne peut connaître d'une voie de recours parce que la sentence a été rendue selon une procédure qui n'est pas celle de la loi du siège, c'est autre chose, remarquait Fouchard [59]. Depuis, la jurisprudence française admet que la régularité d'une sentence internationale, bien que non rattachée à un ordre juridique étatique, est examinée au regard des règles applicables dans le pays où la reconnaissance et l'exécution est demandée [60].

32. Dans la représentation de l'ordre juridique arbitral, le critérium du siège pour répartir les sentences entre nationales ou étrangères est sans pertinence. Cette alternative est remplacée par la distinction entre arbitrage interne ou international, comme l'opère le droit français [61]. La jurisprudence de Singapour adopte dans une affaire *Astro Nusantara* la qualification de «domestic international award» pour justifier l'ouverture d'un recours en exequatur d'une sentence rendue au siège [62].

B. L'articulation entre l'exequatur et l'annulation

33. L'affaire *Astro Nusantara* soulevait l'articulation entre recours en annulation et en exequatur («le double contrôle») au siège de l'arbitrage sur laquelle la Cour suprême de Singapour s'exprime ainsi:

> «. . . we entertain serious doubt as to whether "double-control" extends to the recognition and enforcement of an award which has been set aside in the seat by the court of a foreign jurisdiction. We note that French arbitration law appears to have moved down that path. French law appears to recognise a system of "transnational" or "supranational" arbitral awards, whereby awards do not derive

58. CA Paris, 21 février 1980, *Götaverken*, Aspects philosophiques, par. 66.

59. «Une chose est en effet d'admettre, qu'une procédure arbitrale, surtout dans un arbitrage international, peut échapper totalement à la loi de procédure du pays où elle se déroule; autre chose est d'empêcher la partie condamnée par les arbitres de saisir aussitôt … le juge du lieu où la sentence est rendue et de lui demander de vérifier si cette sentence est régulière. C'est ce juge qui est sans doute, en effet, le mieux placé pour opérer immédiatement cette vérification», *JDI* 1980.660, note Ph. Fouchard.

60. Civ. 1re, 29 juin 2007, no 0518053, *Putrabali*; 8 juillet 2015, no 1352846, *Ryanair*.

61. Articles 1442 ss CPC.

62. *Astro Nusantara* (2014) 1 SLR 372, par. 16, 71.

their validity and legitimacy from a particular local system of law. Thus, in *Hilmarton Ltd* v. *Omnium de traitement et de valorisation* (1995) XX Yearbook Comm Arb 663665 ("Hilmarton"), the Cour de Cassation affirmed the decision of the Cour d'Appel de Paris which declared that the subject award was enforceable in France even though it had been set aside in Switzerland. The Swiss court had annulled the award on the basis that it had misconstrued what constituted an affront to morality in Swiss law (see *Omnium de Traitement et de Valorisation OTV* v. *Hilmarton* (1994) XIX Yearbook Comm Arb 214222). The apex French court held that the Swiss award, being an international award, was not integrated into the legal order of the seat and therefore continued to exist notwithstanding that it had been set aside. The recognition of the award in accordance with French law was not, therefore, contrary to international public policy. The same result and reasoning also features in the Cour d'Appel de Paris' decision of *The Arab Republic of Egypt* v. *Chromalloy Aeroservices, Inc* (1997) XXII Yearbook Comm Arb 691695. France, of course, is not a Model Law jurisdiction and as the Cour de Cassation stated in Hilmarton, the relevant French legislation (Art. 1502 of the New Code of Civil Procedure) does not contain the equivalent of Art. V (1) *(e)* of the New York Convention (the wording of which is identical to Art. 36 (1) *(a) (v)* of the Model Law). . .

While the wording of Article V (1) *(e)* of the New York Convention and Article 36 (1) *(a) (v)* of the Model Law arguably contemplates the possibility that an award which has been set aside may still be enforced, in the sense that the refusal to enforce remains subject to the discretion of the enforcing court, the contemplated *erga omnes* effect of a successful application to set aside an award would generally lead to the conclusion that there is simply no award to enforce. What else could it mean to set aside an award? If this avenue of recourse would only ever be of efficacy in relation to enforcement proceedings in the seat court, then it seems to have been devised for little, if any, discernible purpose. As such, we do not think that in principle, even the wider notion of "doublecontrol" can encompass the same approach as has been adopted by the French courts. The refusal to enforce awards which have not been set aside at the seat court may therefore constitute one of the outerlimits of "double-control". However, as this specific issue is not directly engaged in the present appeal, we offer no further comment beyond these tentative thoughts. » [63]

34. Donnons la parole à Gaillard :

« [l]a croyance selon laquelle l'arbitrage puise la source de sa juridicité exclusivement dans l'ordre juridique du siège a pour conséquence immédiate de rendre impossible, dans tout autre ordre juridique, l'exécution de sentences annulées au siège. Dans cette représentation, la situation est simple. Une sentence annulée au siège n'a plus d'existence légale. Elle ne peut donc être reconnue nulle part. Le modèle westphalien conduit au résultat inverse. Chaque Etat appréciant pour lui-même, selon ses propres conceptions, ce qui constitue une convention d'arbitrage puis une sentence valables, aucun obstacle théorique ne s'oppose à la reconnaissance, dans un Etat, d'une sentence annulée dans un autre ... La représentation qui accepte l'existence d'un ordre juridique arbitral ne conduit pas à un résultat différent. S'agissant en effet d'une question de reconnaissance et d'exécution d'une sentence dans un Etat, il suffit que cette sentence soit détachée de l'ordre juridique du siège pour pouvoir être reconnue ailleurs en dépit de l'annulation qui la frappe au siège » [64].

35. Sa proposition doctrinale est, comme nous le rappelle l'arrêt *Nusantara*, acceptée dans la jurisprudence française [65]. La représentation de l'ordre juridique arbitral n'est pas acceptée par les juridictions de Singapour ou par les juridictions anglaises ainsi que l'établit l'arrêt *Dallah*, où répondant à l'argument de Dallah, semble-t-il inspiré par le rôle réduit du siège, d'un examen plus strict de la compétence arbitrale dans le contexte de l'exécution que dans celui de l'annulation, la Cour suprême britannique dit :

« The concept of transnational arbitration has been advocated in arbitral circles, and was no doubt recognised by French courts, in order so far as possible to underline the autonomy of international

63. *PT First Media TBK (formerly known as PT Broadband Multimedia TBK)* v. *Astro Nusantara International BV* and others and another appeal (2014) 1 SLR 372, par. 76, 77.

64. *Aspects philosophiques*, par. 125.

65. Civ. 1re, 29 juin 2007, n° 0518053, *Putrabali*, en application de l'article VII de la Convention de New York, il est donc possible de se prévaloir des dispositions du droit français de l'arbitrage international qui ne prévoit pas l'annulation de la sentence dans son pays d'origine comme cause de refus de reconnaissance et d'exécution de la sentence rendue à l'étranger.

arbitration from the seat of arbitration or its national legal system. What matters in real terms is where an arbitration award can be enforced : see Gaillard's Legal Theory of International Arbitration, *(op. cit.)* Chapter I. Yet [Dallah's] submissions invoke in one and the same breath a transnational view and a view attaching a special and dominant significance to the law of the seat. They also invite the spectre of dual sets of proceedings, conducted in two different countries (that of the seat and that of enforcement) involving different levels of review in relation to essentially the same issue – whether the award should be enforced in the latter country. »[66]

36. Il n'en reste pas moins que l'on peut trouver, comme dans la jurisprudence de Singapour qui reconnaît le moindre rôle du siège,[67] des traces de la représentation westphalienne dans l'arrêt *Dallah* avec l'admission que «what matters, self-evidently, to both parties is the enforceability of the award in the country where enforcement is sought» en l'absence de toute obligation d'introduire une action en annulation au siège avant de pouvoir contester la compétence du tribunal arbitral lors de l'exequatur[68]. A cet égard, l'affaire *Nusantara* est encore intéressante, cette fois-ci devant les juridictions de Hong Kong, où l'exequatur des sentences a été également recherché. Comme ses homologues britannique et singapourien, le juge hong-kongais reconnaît qu'une critique des sentences est possible en l'absence d'action en annulation au siège[69]. Il faut bien y voir un rejet de la représentation monolocalisatrice selon laquelle, l'arbitrage n'étant pas autonome de l'ordre juridique du siège dont les décisions devraient s'imposer à tous, serait par voie de conséquence irrecevable une action en exequatur si l'annulation n'a pas été demandée[70]. Pour les autres représentations qui rendent possible la renonciation au recours en annulation, la contestation de la sentence n'est évidemment pas liée à l'obligation d'agir en annulation[71].

---

66. *Dallah Real Estate* v. *The Ministry of Religious Affairs, Government of Pakistan*, jugement du 3 novembre 2010 (2010) UKSC 46, par. 27.
67. *Astro Nusantara* (2014) 1 SLR 372, par. 62, 64.
68. *Dallah*, par. 28, 29, 33.
69. *Astro Nusantara* v. *First Media*, 11 avril 2018 (2018) HKCFA 12, par. 75, 78. A. Reyes, The Practice of International Commercial Arbitration, A Handbook for Hong Kong Arbitrators, Informa Law from Routledge, 2018, p. 173.
70. E. Gaillard, «Souveraineté et autonomie : réflexions sur les représentations de l'arbitrage international», *JDI* 2007.1163, n° 20.
71. Article 192 LDIP, article 1717 alinéa 4 Code judiciaire belge, article 51 loi suédoise sur l'arbitrage, article 1522 alinéa 1 CPC.

37. La représentation plurilocalisatrice et celle de l'ordre juridique arbitral se refusent à remettre le sort de la sentence entre les mains de l'ordre juridique du siège : pour la première, chaque Etat apprécie pour lui-même les conditions de validité de la sentence, pour la seconde, la sentence continue d'exister en dehors de sa non-reconnaissance par un ordre juridique étatique particulier puisqu'elle relève d'un tiers ordre juridique [72]. L'exemple le plus fameux nous est fourni par la jurisprudence *Putrabali* de la Cour de cassation française pour laquelle la sentence internationale, n'étant rattachée à aucun ordre juridique étatique, est une décision de justice internationale dont la régularité est examinée au regard des règles applicables dans le pays où sa reconnaissance et son exécution sont demandées [73].

C. Le rôle des jugements dans le contrôle des sentences

38. La représentation monolocalisatrice, observe Gaillard, qui subordonne l'arbitrage aux juridictions étatiques, produit l'effet pervers de contrôler la reconnaissance des décisions qui se prononcent sur le sort de la sentence plutôt que d'affronter le débat sur la réalisation des conditions d'exequatur de la sentence elle-même, telles que prévues par la Convention de New York [74]. Il écrit à propos de ce regain de courtoisie internationale :

> « [c]ela signifie, paradoxalement, que plus l'esprit d'internationalité est fort, et donc plus la barre est haute pour refuser de donner effet à un jugement étranger, moins la sentence querellée bénéficiera de cet esprit d'ouverture » [75].

39. Il s'agit au premier chef des décisions d'annulation de la sentence. L'arrêt *Nusantara* de Singapour cite Gaillard [76] qui avait souligné, à propos du double exequatur condamné par la Convention de New York, combien exercer un contrôle de la décision étrangère ayant statué sur la validité de la sentence au regard des règles applicables aux jugements étrangers opère une rupture avec cette Convention qui

72. *Aspects philosophiques*, par. 124 ss.
73. Civ. 1re, 29 juin 2007, no 0518053, *Putrabali.*
74. Souveraineté et autonomie : réflexions sur les représentations de l'arbitrage international, JDI 2007.1163, no 13.
75. *Rev. arb.* 2019.1151.
76. Par. 62.

invite les juridictions ayant à se prononcer sur la reconnaissance ou l'exécution de la sentence à raisonner directement sur la sentence [77].

40. L'affaire *Bechtel* devant la Cour d'appel de Paris, illustre le propos de Gaillard. Le débat portait sur la contrariété à l'ordre public de l'arrêt de la Cour de cassation de Dubaï annulant la sentence, en raison du manque d'indépendance de la justice à Dubaï. Il était soutenu que la justice dubaïote aurait voulu complaire aux pouvoirs publics locaux dans une affaire où l'Etat débiteur de la sentence était maître d'ouvrage de la construction litigieuse. Il est répondu que les décisions rendues dans une instance en annulation

> «ne produisent pas d'effets internationaux, car elles ne concernent qu'une souveraineté déterminée sur le territoire où elle s'exerce, aucune appréciation ne pouvant être portée sur ces décisions émises par un juge étranger à l'occasion d'un procès indirect» [78].

D'autres ordres juridiques sont prêts à partager le point de vue selon lequel une sentence annulée pour des motifs nationaux, tels dans l'affaire *Bechtel*, l'audition des témoins sans un serment prêté dans les formes de la procédure civile locale, devrait être néanmoins considérée pour son exécution ailleurs qu'au siège.

41. A l'inverse, il y a d'autres juridictions qui ont accepté de se prononcer sur la régularité internationale du jugement d'annulation pour en tirer des conséquences sur l'exécution de la sentence. La contrariété à l'ordre public de la décision du juge de l'annulation leur a alors permis d'ordonner l'exécution de la sentence [79].

42. L'autorité de chose jugée du jugement qui rejette un grief contre la sentence peut-elle donner lieu à une fin de non-recevoir pour ce même grief devant un autre juge? Dans la représentation de l'ordre juridique arbitral, la réponse est clairement négative, chaque ordre juridique étatique s'exprime de manière autonome [80]. De même, dans la représentation westphalienne, chaque Etat doit pouvoir s'exprimer sur la

---

77. *Aspects philosophiques*, par. 131.

78. CA Paris, 29 septembre 2005, Rev. arb. 2006.695, note H. Muir Watt; *Rev. crit. DIP* 2006.387, note A. Szekely.

79. CA Amsterdam, 28 avril 2009, Rev arb. 2009.557, note S. Bollée; E. Gaillard, «La vision américaine des sentences annulées au siège», *Rev. arb.* 2017.1147. Aspects philosophiques, par. 128.

80. CA Paris, 12 février 1993, *Rev. arb.* 1993.255 et la note (la décision du Tribunal fédéral suisse de rejet d'annulation ne peut supprimer ou exclure le contrôle par le juge de l'exequatur). Cl. Debourg, *Les contrariétés de décisions dans l'arbitrage international*, LGDJ, 2012.

sentence sans être lié par la vision des autres [81]. Mais laissons s'exprimer le juge anglais sur l'exequatur d'une sentence dont l'exécution avait déjà été disputée devant un juge étranger. A l'exception près de l'ordre public que chaque juge est dans l'obligation de vérifier au regard de ses propres conceptions [82], les portes sont ouvertes à la fin de non-recevoir de la chose jugée par un précédent juge de l'exequatur :

> « However, in circumstances where a foreign court decides that an award is not "binding", I see no reason in principle why that decision should not give rise to an issue estoppel between the parties provided, of course, that the other conditions referred to above apply. In particular, provided that the issue is the same and that the decision can properly be said to be "on the merits", it does not seem to me that the fact that such decision was made in the context of enforcement proceedings as opposed to any other type of proceedings can, of itself, be material. Indeed, that is consistent with the view expressed in the leading textbook, Dicey, Morris & Collins, The Conflict of Laws, 15 th Ed para. 14-122 referring to *Owens Bank* v. *Bracco* [1992] 2 AC 443 at pp. 470-F-472E and *House of Spring Gardens Ltd.* v. *Waite* [1991] QB 241. It also seems implicit in the decision of the Court of Appeal in *Yukos Capital* v. *Rosneft.* » [83]

---

81. *Aspects philosophiques*, par. 34.

82. *Yukos Capital* v. *Rosneft* [2012] EWCA Civ 855 sur l'exequatur de la sentence rendue dans l'affaire *Youkos* au sujet de la décision du juge néerlandais qui avait précédemment écarté, pour accorder l'exequatur aux Pays-Bas, le jugement d'annulation russe prononcé dans un contexte juridictionnel partial et dépendant :

> « The difficulty . . . is that "public order" or "public policy" is inevitably different in each country. The standards by which any particular country resolves the question whether the courts of another country are "partial and dependent" may vary considerably and it is also a matter of high policy to determine the circumstances in which this country should recognise the judgments of a state where the interests of that very state are at stake. Normally such recognition will be given and, if it is to be refused, cogent evidence of partiality and dependency will be required. Our own law is (or may be) that considerations of comity necessitate specific examples of partiality and dependency before any decision is made not to recognise the judgments of a foreign state. It is our own public order which defines the framework of any assessment of this difficult question ; whether such decisions are truly to be regarded as dependent and partial as a matter of English law is not the same question as whether such decisions are to be regarded as dependent and partial in the view of some other court according to that court's notions of what is acceptable or otherwise according to its law », par. 151.

83. *Diag Human* v. *The Czech Republic* [2014] EWHC 1639 (Comm), par. 59.

43. Prêtons attention à Gaillard: la coopération internationale qui se développe entre juridictions étatiques à propos de l'arbitrage révèle une réelle difficulté à reconnaître dans les arbitres de véritables juges. Même si cela peut aboutir à donner effet à la sentence, lancer un forum shopping entre les juridictions étatiques selon le résultat escompté du contrôle de la sentence, amplifie une vision territorialiste de l'arbitrage centrée sur l'ordre juridique du siège et s'éloigne de la représentation plurilocalisatrice qui confie la sentence à l'ensemble des ordres juridiques nationaux prêts à la reconnaître [84]. Certes, l'effet de chose jugée d'un jugement qui valide la sentence empêche de rouvrir le débat sur les mêmes griefs. Mais l'harmonie des solutions à laquelle on parvient repose entièrement sur les aléas de l'entraide judiciaire [85]. Elle s'inscrit dans une vision monolocalisatrice avec l'idée que les parties ont implicitement accepté les décisions des juridictions du siège en soumettant l'arbitrage à l'ordre juridique du for [86]. On en trouve une trace dans un ancien arrêt de la Cour de cassation pour lequel l'interdiction de la révision au fond du jugement anglais ayant validé la sentence s'opposait à toute nouvelle discussion devant le juge de l'exequatur [87]. L'harmonie par le dialogue entre ordres juridiques étatiques et avec l'ordre juridique arbitral, qui caractérise les autres représentations, pour dégager des principes partagés sur le règlement des différends internationaux y trouve peu son compte.

44. En conclusion, et avec toute la prudence sur laquelle insiste Gaillard à la fin de son cours sur le sens de l'évolution, on peut observer qu'à ce stade, la représentation westphalienne s'installe majoritairement dans les décisions de justice, même si la vision monolocalisatrice persiste dans le traitement des voies de recours par les juges. On peut être tenté de l'expliquer parce que le point de vue westphalien est à la fois le plus libre et le plus discrétionnaire. Il devrait donc se développer par la prise de conscience des juridictions, qui le pratiquent déjà, pour en étendre les conséquences. En comparaison, le juge qui épouse la représentation de l'ordre juridique arbitral est soumis à de plus grandes exigences. Plus ambitieuse, cette vision nécessite en effet

---

84. E. Gaillard, «Dialogue des ordres juridiques: ordre juridique arbitral et ordres juridiques étatiques», *Rev. arb.* 2018.493.

85. E. Gaillard, «Coordination or Chaos: Do the Principles of Comity, *Lis Pendens*, and *Res Judicata* Apply to International Arbitration?», *American Review of International Law*, vol. 29, n° 3, 2018, p. 205; *The Myth of Harmony in International Arbitration*, 2018 Lalive Lecture, ICSID Review, vol. 34, n° 3 (2019), p. 553-558.

86. Lord Mance, 30th Freshfields Arbitration Lecture, 4 novembre 2015, par. 15.

87. Cass. civ. 1re, 11 janvier 1972, *Rev. arb.* 1972.49 (2e arrêt), note E. Mezger.

un exigeant travail de droit comparé, à l'instar du travail de l'arbitre mené avec l'aide des parties, pour mettre en valeur des règles adoptées par la collectivité des Etats et montrer l'existence d'une normativité commune [88]. Apportant le point de vue de l'arbitre [89], la représentation de l'ordre juridique arbitral représente un défi plus ambitieux pour le juge, surtout quand celui-ci n'a aucune expérience concrète de l'arbitrage. L'exigence de cohérence dans le développement des règles jurisprudentielles est aussi plus grande avec la vision de l'ordre juridique arbitral. Il peut y avoir des retours [90], des ajustements [91], mais l'adhésion à la représentation de l'ordre juridique arbitral implique une expansion maîtrisée pour développer de nouvelles règles matérielles et non un point de vue statique dont peut, en comparaison, se contenter la représentation monolocalisatrice.

45. Plus modestement enfin, mais c'est déjà beaucoup, les représentations de l'arbitrage aiguillonnent les juges à entreprendre une démarche d'ouverture et de dialogue sur leurs jurisprudences respectives, ce dont on pourrait escompter une compréhension améliorée des solutions qu'ils choisissent pour sécuriser l'arbitrage. Le plus important, c'est bien la représentation.

88. *Aspects philosophiques*, par. 60. E. Gaillard, « Comparative Law in International Arbitration, *Jus Comparatum* (2020) », p. 1-35 (International Academy of Comparative Law).

89. « Par rapport à la précédente, cette représentation consiste essentiellement à intégrer le point de vue des arbitres … D'une représentation monolocalisatrice de l'arbitrage centrée sur la notion du siège, on est ainsi passé à une représentation multilocalisatrice (ou westphalienne), puis à une représentation transnationale de l'arbitrage qui ne conçoit plus chaque Etat de manière isolée mais qui se préoccupe des tendances susceptibles de découler de l'activité normative de la communauté des Etats. C'est dans le passage du pluriel au collectif que tient l'opposition entre la deuxième et la troisième des représentations de l'arbitrage… » L'ordre juridique arbitral est « … entièrement fondé sur l'activité normative des Etats, qu'il appréhende de manière globale et non comme une juxtaposition de droits ne pouvant être départagés qu'à l'aide d'une règle de conflit », Aspects philosophiques du droit de l'arbitrage international, Adi-Poche, Martinus Nijhoff Publishers, 2008, par. 41, 50. M. Schinazi, The Three Ages of International Commercial Arbitration, Cambridge Studies in International and Comparative Law, CUP, 2022.

90. Cass. civ. 1re, 30 mars 2004, nº 0114311 (rôle résiduel de la loi applicable à la convention d'arbitrage).

91. Cass. civ. 1re, 30 septembre 2020, nº 1819241 pour une adaptation de la règle de priorité en matière d'arbitrage de la consommation et à l'accès à l'arbitrage.

PUBLICATIONS DE L'ACADÉMIE
DE DROIT INTERNATIONAL
DE LA HAYE

PUBLICATIONS OF THE
HAGUE ACADEMY OF INTERNATIONAL
LAW

RECUEIL DES COURS

Depuis 1923, les plus grands noms du droit international ont professé à l'Académie de droit international de La Haye. Tous les tomes du *Recueil* qui ont été publiés depuis cette date sont disponibles, chaque tome étant, depuis les tout premiers, régulièrement réimprimé sous sa forme originale.

Depuis 2008, certains cours font l'objet d'une édition en livres de poche.

En outre, toute la collection existe en version électronique. Tous les ouvrages parus à ce jour ont été mis en ligne et peuvent être consultés moyennant un des abonnements proposés, qui offrent un éventail de tarifs et de possibilités.

INDEX

A ce jour, il a paru sept index généraux. Ils couvrent les tomes suivants :

1 à 101	(1923-1960)	379 pages	ISBN 978-90-218-9948-0
102 à 125	(1961-1968)	204 pages	ISBN 978-90-286-0643-2
126 à 151	(1969-1976)	280 pages	ISBN 978-90-286-0630-2
152 à 178	(1976-1982)	416 pages	ISBN 978-0-7923-2955-8
179 à 200	(1983-1986)	260 pages	ISBN 978-90-411-0110-5
201 à 250	(1987-1994)	448 pages	ISBN 978-90-04-13700-4
251 à 300	(1995-2002)	580 pages	ISBN 978-90-04-15387-7

A partir du tome 210 il a été décidé de publier un index complet qui couvrira chaque fois dix tomes du *Recueil des cours*. Le dernier index paru couvre les tomes suivants :

311 à 320 (2004-2006) 392 pages Tome 320A ISBN 978-90-04-19695-7

COLLOQUES

L'Académie organise également des colloques dont les débats sont publiés. Les derniers volumes parus de ces colloques portent les titres suivants : *Le règlement pacifique des différends internationaux en Europe : perspectives d'avenir* (1990) ; *Le développement du rôle du Conseil de sécurité* (1992) ; *La Convention sur l'interdiction et l'élimination des armes chimiques : une percée dans l'entreprise multilatérale du désarmement* (1994) ; *Actualité de la Conférence de La Haye de 1907, Deuxième Conférence de la Paix* (2007).

CENTRE D'ÉTUDE ET DE RECHERCHE

Les travaux scientifiques du Centre d'étude et de recherche de droit international et de relations internationales de l'Académie de droit international de La Haye, dont les sujets sont choisis par le Curatorium de l'Académie, faisaient l'objet, depuis la session de 1985, d'une publication dans laquelle les directeurs d'études dressaient le bilan des recherches du Centre qu'ils avaient dirigé. Cette série a été arrêtée et la dernière brochure parue porte le titre suivant : *Les règles et les institutions du droit international humanitaire à l'épreuve des conflits armés récents*. Néanmoins, lorsque les travaux du Centre se révèlent particulièrement intéressants et originaux, les rapports des directeurs et les articles rédigés par les chercheurs font l'objet d'un ouvrage collectif.

Les demandes de renseignements ou de catalogues et les commandes doivent être adressées à

MARTINUS NIJHOFF PUBLISHERS

B.P. 9000, 2300 PA Leyde Pays-Bas **http://www.brill.nl**

COLLECTED COURSES

Since 1923 the top names in international law have taught at The Hague Academy of International Law. All the volumes of the *Collected Courses* which have been published since 1923 are available, as, since the very first volume, they are reprinted regularly in their original format.

Since 2008, certain courses have been the subject of a pocketbook edition.

In addition, the total collection now exists in electronic form. All works already published have been put "on line" and can be consulted under one of the proposed subscription methods, which offer a range of tariffs and possibilities.

INDEXES

Up till now seven General Indexes have been published. They cover the following volumes:

1 to 101	(1923-1960)	379 pages	ISBN 978-90-218-9948-0
102 to 125	(1961-1968)	204 pages	ISBN 978-90-286-0643-2
126 to 151	(1969-1976)	280 pages	ISBN 978-90-286-0630-2
152 to 178	(1976-1982)	416 pages	ISBN 978-0-7923-2955-8
179 to 200	(1983-1986)	260 pages	ISBN 978-90-411-0110-5
201 to 250	(1987-1994)	448 pages	ISBN 978-90-04-13700-4
251 to 300	(1995-2002)	580 pages	ISBN 978-90-04-15387-7

From Volume 210 onwards it has been decided to publish a full index covering, each time, ten volumes of the *Collected Courses*. The latest Index published covers the following volumes:

311 to 320 (2004-2006) 392 pages Volume 320A ISBN 978-90-04-19695-7

WORKSHOPS

The Academy publishes the discussions from the Workshops which it organises. The latest titles of the Workshops already published are as follows: *The Peaceful Settlement of International Disputes in Europe: Future Prospects* (1990) ; *The Development of the Role of the Security Council* (1992); *The Convention on the Prohibition and Elimination of Chemical Weapons: A Breakthrough in Multilateral Disarmament* (1994); *Topicality of the 1907 Hague Conference, the Second Peace Conference* (2007).

CENTRE FOR STUDIES AND RESEARCH

The scientific works of the Centre for Studies and Research in International Law and International Relations of The Hague Academy of International Law, the subjects of which are chosen by the Curatorium of the Academy, have been published, since the Centre's 1985 session, in a publication in which the Directors of Studies reported on the state of research of the Centre under their direction. This series has been discontinued and the title of the latest booklet published is as follows: *Rules and Institutions of International Humanitarian Law Put to the Test of Recent Armed Conflicts.* Nevertheless, when the work of the Centre has been of particular interest and originality, the reports of the Directors of Studies together with the articles by the researchers form the subject of a collection published by the Academy.

Requests for information, catalogues and orders for publications must be addressed to

MARTINUS NIJHOFF PUBLISHERS

P.O. Box 9000, 2300 PA Leiden The Netherlands **http://www.brill.nl**

TABLE PAR TOME DES COURS PUBLIÉS CES DERNIÈRES ANNÉES

INDEX BY VOLUME OF THE COURSES PUBLISHED THESE LAST YEARS

Tome/Volume 308 (2004)

Rigo Sureda, A. : The Law Applicable to the Activities of International Development Banks, 9-252.
González Lapeyre, E. : Transport maritime et régime portuaire, 253-378.
(ISBN 978-90-04-14547-4)

Tome/Volume 309 (2004)

Karaquillo, J.-P. : Droit international du sport, 9-124.
Maresceau, M. : Bilateral Agreements Concluded by the European Community, 9-452.
(ISBN 978-90-04-14548-1)

Tome/Volume 310 (2004)

Kamto, M. : La volonté de l'Etat en droit international, 9-428.
(ISBN 978-90-04-14552-8)

Tome/Volume 311 (2004)

Struycken, A. V. M. : Co-ordination and Co-operation in Respectful Disagreement. General Course on Private International Law, 5-552.
(ISBN 978-90-04-14553-5)

Tome/Volume 312 (2005)

Gaudemet-Tallon, H. : Le pluralisme en droit international privé : richesses et faiblesses (Le funambule et l'arc-en-ciel). Cours général, 9-488.
(ISBN 978-90-04-14554-2)

Tome/Volume 313 (2005)

Mani, V. S. : "Humanitarian" Intervention Today, 9-324.
David, E. : La Cour pénale internationale, 325-454.
(ISBN 978-90-04-14555-9)

Tome/Volume 314 (2005)

Draetta, U. : Internet et commerce électronique en droit international des affaires, 9-232.
Daillier, P. : Les opérations multinationales consécutives à des conflits armés en vue du rétablissement de la paix, 233-432.
(ISBN 978-90-04-14557-3)

Tome/Volume 315 (2005)

Dogauchi, M. : Four-Step Analysis of Private International Law, 9-140.
Mohamed Salah, M. M. : Loi d'autonomie et méthodes de protection de la partie faible en droit international privé, 141-264.
Radicati di Brozolo, L. G. : Arbitrage commercial international et lois de police. Considérations sur les conflits de juridictions dans le commerce international, 265-502.
(ISBN 978-90-04-14558-0)

Tome/Volume 316 (2005)

Cançado Trindade, A. A. : International Law for Humankind : Towards a New *Jus Gentium* (I). General Course on Public International Law, 9-440.
(ISBN 978-90-04-15375-2)

Tome/Volume 317 (2005)

Cançado Trindade, A. A. : International Law for Humankind : Towards a New *Jus Gentium* (II). General Course on Public International Law, 9-312.
Borrás, A. : Le droit international privé communautaire : réalités, problèmes et perspectives d'avenir, 313-536.
(ISBN 978-90-04-15376-9)

Tome/Volume 318 (2005)

Kinsch, P. : Droits de l'homme, droits fondamentaux et droit international privé, 9-332.
Bothe, M. : Environment, Development, Resources, 323-516.
(ISBN 978-90-04-15377-6)

Tome/Volume 319 (2006)

Hartley, T. C. : The Modern Approach to Private International Law. International Litigation and Transactions from a Common-Law Perspective. General Course on Private International Law, 9-324.
Crawford, J. : Multilateral Rights and Obligations in International Law, 325-482.
(ISBN 978-90-04-15378-3)

Tome/Volume 320 (2006)

Goldstein, G. : La cohabitation hors mariage en droit international privé, 9-390.
(ISBN 978-90-04-15379-0)

Tome/Volume 321 (2006)

Shaker, M. I. : The Evolving International Regime of Nuclear Non-Proliferation, 9-202.
Klein, P. : Le droit international à l'épreuve du terrorisme, 203-484.
(ISBN 978-90-04-16100-0)

Tome/Volume 322 (2006)

Loquin, E. : Les règles matérielles internationales, 9-242.
Dinstein, Y. : The Interaction between Customary International Law and Treaties, 243-428. (ISBN 978-90-04-16101-6)

Tome/Volume 323 (2006)

Fernández Arroyo, D. P. : Compétence exclusive et compétence exorbitante dans les relations privées internationales, 9-260.
Silberman, L. J.. : Co-operative Efforts in Private International Law on Behalf of Children : The Hague Children's Conventions, 261-478.
(ISBN 978-90-04-16102-3)

Tome/Volume 324 (2006)

Bedjaoui, M. : L'humanité en quête de paix et de développement (I). Cours général de droit international public, 9-530.
(ISBN 978-90-04-16103-0)

Tome/Volume 325 (2006)

Bedjaoui, M. : L'humanité en quête de paix et de développement (II). Cours général de droit international public, 9-542.
(ISBN 978-90-04-16104-7)

Tome/Volume 326 (2007)

Collins, L. : Revolution and Restitution : Foreign States in National Courts (Opening Lecture, Private International Law Session, 2007), 9-72.
Gotanda, J. Y. : Damages in Private International Law, 73-408.
(ISBN 978-90-04-16616-5)

Tome/Volume 327 (2007)

Mayer, P. : Le phénomène de la coordination des ordres juridiques étatiques en droit privé. Cours général de droit international privé (2003), 9-378.
(ISBN 978-90-04-16617-2)

Tome/Volume 328 (2007)

Garcimartín Alférez, F. J., Cross-border Listed Companies, 9-174.
Vrellis, S., Conflit ou coordination de valeurs en droit international privé. A la recherche de la justice, 175-486.
(ISBN 978-90-04-16618-9)

Tome/Volume 329 (2007)

Pellet, A. : L'adaptation du droit international aux besoins changeants de la société internationale (conférence inaugurale, session de droit international public, 2007), 9-48.
Gaillard, E. : Aspects philosophiques du droit de l'arbitrage international, 49-216.
Schrijver, N. : The Evolution of Sustainable Development in International Law : Inception, Meaning and Status, 217-412.
(ISBN 978-90-04-16619-6)

Tome/Volume 330 (2007)

Pamboukis, Ch. P. : Droit international privé holistique : droit uniforme et droit international privé, 9-474. (ISBN 978-90-04-16620-2)

Tome/Volume 331 (2007)

Pinto, M. : L'emploi de la force dans la jurisprudence des tribunaux internationaux, 9-160
Brown Weiss, E. : The Evolution of International Water Law, 161-404.
(ISBN 978-90-04-17288-3)

Tome/Volume 332 (2007)

Carlier, J.-Y. : Droit d'asile et des réfugiés. De la protection aux droits, 9-354.
Fatouros, A. A. : An International Legal Framework for Energy, 355-446.
(ISBN 978-90-04-17198-5)

Tome/Volume 333 (2008)

Müllerson, R. : Democracy Promotion : Institutions, International Law and Politics, 9-174.
Pisillo Mazzeschi, R. : Responsabilité de l'Etat pour violation des obligations positives relatives aux droits de l'homme, 174-506.
(ISBN 978-90-04-17284-5)

Tome/Volume 334 (2008)

Verhoeven, J. : Considérations sur ce qui est commun. Cours général de droit international public (2002), 9-434. (ISBN 978-90-04-17289-0)

Tome/Volume 335 (2008)

Beaumont, P. R.: The Jurisprudence of the European Court of Human Rights and the European Court of Justice on the Hague Convention on International Child Abduction, 9-104.

Moura Vicente, D.: La propriété intellectuelle en droit international privé, 105-504. (ISBN 978-90-04-17290-6)

Tome/Volume 336 (2008)

Decaux, E.: Les formes contemporaines de l'esclavage, 9-198.

McLachlan, C.: *Lis Pendens* in International Litigation, 199-554. (ISBN 978-90-04-17291-3)

Tome/Volume 337 (2008)

Mahiou, A.: Le droit international ou la dialectique de la rigueur et de la flexibilité. Cours général de droit international public, 9-516. (ISBN 978-90-04-17292-0)

Tome/Volume 338 (2008)

Thürer, D.: International Humanitariam Law : Theory, Practice, Context, 9-370. (ISBN 978-90-04-17293-7)

Tome/Volume 339 (2008)

Sicilianos, L.-A.: Entre multilatéralisme et unilatéralisme : l'autorisation par le Conseil de sécurité de recourir à la force, 9-436. (ISBN 978-90-04-17294-4)

Tome/Volume 340 (2009)

Beaumont, P. R.: Reflections on the Relevance of Public International Law to Private International Law Treaty Making (Opening Lecture, Private International Law Session, 2009), 9-62.

Carbone, S. M.: Conflits de lois en droit maritime, 63-270.

Boele-Woelki, K.: Unifying and Harmonizing Substantive Law and the Role of Conflict of Laws, 271-462. (ISBN 978-90-04-17295-1)

Tome/Volume 341 (2009)

Bucher, A.: La dimension sociale du droit international privé. Cours général, 9-526. (ISBN 978-90-04-18509-8)

Tome/Volume 342 (2009)

Musin, V.: The Influence of the International Sale of Goods Convention on Domestic Law Including Conflict of Laws (with Specific Reference to Russian Law), 9-76.

Onuma, Y.: A Transcivilizational Perspective on International Law. Questioning Prevalent Cognitive Frameworks in the Emerging Multi-Polar and Multi-Civilizational World of the Twenty-First Century, 77-418. (ISBN 978-90-04-18510-4)

Tome/Volume 343 (2009)

Abou-el-Wafa, A.: Les différends internationaux concernant les frontières terrestres dans la jurisprudence de la Cour internationale de Justice, 9-570.
(ISBN 978-90-04-18513-5)

Tome/Volume 344 (2009)

Villiger, M. E.: The 1969 Vienna Convention on the Law of Treaties – 40 Years After, 4-192.
Alvarez, J. E.: The Public International Law Regime Governing International Investment, 193-452. (ISBN 978-90-04-18512-8)

Tome/Volume 345 (2009)

Meziou, K.: Migrations et relations familiales, 9-386.
Lauterpacht, Sir Elihu: Principles of Procedure in International Litigation, 387-530. (ISBN 978-90-04-18514-2)

Tome/Volume 346 (2009)

Kawano, M.: The Role of Judicial Procedures in the Process of the Pacific Settlement of International Disputes, 9-474. (ISBN 978-90-04-18515-9)

Tome/Volume 347 (2010)

Salmon, J.: Quelle place pour l'Etat dans le droit international d'aujourd'hui? 9-78.
Boisson de Chazournes, L.: Les relations entre organisations régionales et organisations universelles, 79-406.
(ISBN 978-90-04-18516-6)

Tome/Volume 348 (2010)

Bogdan, M.: Private International Law as Component of the Law of the Forum. General Course, 9-252.
Baratta, R.: La reconnaissance internationale des situations juridiques personnelles et familiales, 253-500.
(ISBN 978-90-04-18517-3)

Tome/Volume 349 (2010)

Malenovský, J.: L'indépendance des juges internationaux, 9-276.
Wang, G.: Radiating Impact of WTO on Its Members' Legal System: The Chinese Perspective, 277-536. (ISBN 978-90-04-18518-0)

Tome/Volume 350 (2010)

Van Gerven, W.: Plaidoirie pour une nouvelle branche du droit: le «droit des conflits d'ordres juridiques» dans le prolongement du «droit des conflits de règles» (conférence inaugurale), 9-70.
Bonomi, A.: Successions internationales: conflits de lois et de juridictions, 71-418.
Oxman, B. H.: Idealism and the Study of International Law (Inaugural Lecture), 419-440. (ISBN 978-90-04-18519-7)

Tome/Volume 351 (2010)

Reisman, W. M.: The Quest for World Order and Human Dignity in the Twenty-first Century: Constitutive Process and Individual Commitment. General Course on Public International Law, 9-382.
(ISBN 978-90-04-22725-5)

Tome/Volume 352 (2010)

Daví, A.: Le renvoi en droit international privé contemporain, 9-522.

(ISBN 978-90-04-22726-2)

Tome/Volume 353 (2011)

Meeusen, J.: Le droit international privé et le principe de non-discrimination, 9-184.

Gowlland-Debbas, V.: The Security Council and Issues of Responsibility under International Law, 185-444.

(ISBN 978-90-04-22727-9)

Tome/Volume 354 (2011)

Lamm, C. B.: Internationalization of the Practice of Law and Important Emerging Issues for Investor-State Arbitration (Opening Lecture), 9-64.

Briggs, A.: The Principle of Comity in Private International Law, 65-182.

Davey, W. J.: Non-discrimination in the World Trade Organization: The Rules and Exceptions, 183-440.

(ISBN 978-90-04-22728-6)

Tome/Volume 355 (2011)

Chemillier-Gendreau, M.: A quelles conditions l'universalité du droit international est-elle possible? (conférence inaugurale), 9-40.

Xue Hanqin: Chinese Contemporary Perspectives on International Law – History, Culture and International Law, 41-234.

Arrighi, J. M.: L'Organisation des Etats américains et le droit international, 235-438.

(ISBN 978-90-04-22729-3)

Tome/Volume 356 (2011)

Talpis, J.: Succession Substitutes, 9-238.

Lagrange, E.: L'efficacité des normes internationales concernant la situation des personnes privées dans les ordres juridiques internes, 239-552.

(ISBN 978-90-04-22730-9)

Tome/Volume 357 (2011)

Dugard, J.: The Secession of States and Their Recognition in the Wake of Kosovo, 9-222.

Gannagé, L.: Les méthodes du droit international privé à l'épreuve des conflits de cultures, 223-490.

(ISBN 978-90-04-22731-6)

Tome/Volume 358 (2011)

Brand, R. A.: Transaction Planning Using Rules on Jurisdiction and the Recognition and Enforcement of Judgments, 9-262.

Hafner, G.: The Emancipation of the Individual from the State under International Law, 263-454.

(ISBN 978-90-04-22732-3)

Tome/Volume 359 (2012)

Opertti Badán, D.: Conflit de lois et droit uniforme dans le droit international privé contemporain: dilemme ou convergence? (conférence inaugurale), 9-86.

Chen Weizuo: La nouvelle codification du droit international privé chinois, 87-234.

Kohler, Ch.: L'autonomie de la volonté en droit international privé: un principe universel entre libéralisme et étatisme, 285-478.

(ISBN 978-90-04-25541-8)

Tome/Volume 360 (2012)

Basedow, J.: The Law of Open Societies — Private Ordering and Public Regulation of International Relations. General Course on Private International Law, 9-516.
(ISBN 978-90-04-25550-0)

Tome/Volume 361 (2012)

Pinto, M. C. W.: The Common Heritage of Mankind: Then and Now, 9-130.
Kreindler, R.: Competence-Competence in the Face of Illegality in Contracts and Arbitration Agreements, 131-482.
(ISBN 978-90-04-25552-4)

Tome/Volume 362 (2012)

Arsanjani, M. H.: The United Nations and International Law-Making (Opening Lecture), 9-40.
Alland, D.: L'interprétation du droit international public, 41-394.
(ISBN 978-90-04-25554-8)

Tome/Volume 363 (2012)

Sur, S.: La créativité du droit international. Cours général de droit international public, 9-332.
Turp, D.: La contribution du droit international au maintien de la diversité culturelle, 333-454. (ISBN 978-90-04-25556-2)

Tome/Volume 364 (2012)

Gaja, G.: The Protection of General Interests in the International Community. General Course on Public International Law (2011), 9-186.
Glenn, H. P.: La conciliation des lois. Cours général de droit international privé (2011), 187-470.
(ISBN 978-90-04-25557-9)

Tome/Volume 365 (2013)

Crawford, J.: Chance, Order, Change: The Course of International Law. General Course on Public International Law, 9-390.
(ISBN 978-90-04-25560-9)

Tome/Volume 366 (2013)

Hayton, D.: "Trusts" in Private International Law, 9-98.
Hobér, K.: *Res Judicata* and *Lis Pendens* in International Arbitration, 99-406.
(ISBN 978-90-04-26395-6)

Tome/Volume 367 (2013)

Kolb, R.: L'article 103 de la Charte des Nations Unies, 9-252.
Nascimbene, B.: Le droit de la nationalité et le droit des organisations d'intégration régionales. Vers de nouveaux statuts de résidents ?, 253-454.
(ISBN 978-90-04-26793-0)

Tome/Volume 368 (2013)

Caflisch, L: Frontières nationales, limites et délimitations. – Quelle importance aujourd'hui ? (conférence inaugurale), 9-46.
Benvenisti, E.: The International Law of Global Governance, 47-280.
Park, K. G.: La protection des personnes en cas de catastrophes, 281-456.
(ISBN 978-90-04-26795-4)

Tome/Volume 369 (2013)

Kronke, H.: Transnational Commercial Law and Conflict of Laws: Institutional Co-operation and Substantive Complementarity (Opening Lecture), 9-42.
Ortiz Ahlf, L.: The Human Rights of Undocumented Migrants, 43-160.
Kono, T.: Efficiency in Private International Law, 161-360.
Yusuf, A. A.: Pan-Africanism and International Law, 361-512.
(ISBN 978-90-04-26797-8)

Tome/Volume 370 (2013)

Dominicé, Ch.: La société internationale à la recherche de son équilibre. Cours général de droit international public, 9-392. (ISBN 978-90-04-26799-2)

Tome/Volume 371 (2014)

Lagarde, P.: La méthode de la reconnaissance est-elle l'avenir du droit international privé ?, 9-42.
Charlesworth, H.: Democracy and International Law, 43-152.
de Vareilles-Sommières, P.: L'exception d'ordre public et la régularité substantielle internationale de la loi étrangère, 153-272.
Yanagihara, M.: Significance of the History of the Law of Nations in Europe and East Asia, 273-435. (ISBN 978-90-04-28936-9)

Tome/Volume 372 (2014)

Bucher, A.: La compétence universelle civile, 9-128.
Cordero-Moss, G.: Limitations on Party Autonomy in International Commercial Arbitration, 129-326.
Sinjela, M.: Intellectual Property: Cross-Border Recognition of Rights and National Development, 327-394.
Dolzer, R.: International Co-operation in Energy Affairs, 395-504.
(ISBN 978-90-04-28937-6)

Tome/Volume 373 (2014)

Cachard, O.: Le transport international aérien de passagers, 9-216.
Audit, M.: Bioéthique et droit international privé, 217-447.
(ISBN 978-90-04-28938-3)

Tome/Volume 374 (2014)

Struycken, A. V. M.: Arbitration and State Contract, 9-52.
Corten, O., La rébellion et le droit international : le principe de neutralité en tension, 53-312.
Parra, A.: The Convention and Centre for Settlement of Investment Disputes, 313-410. (ISBN 978-90-04-29764-7)

Tome/Volume 375 (2014)

Jayme, E.: Narrative Norms in Private International Law – The Example of Art Law, 9-52.
De Boer, Th. M.: Choice of Law in Arbitration Proceedings, 53-88.
Frigo, M.: Circulation des biens culturels, détermination de la loi applicable et méthodes de règlement des litiges, 89-474. (ISBN 978-90-04-29766-1)

Tome/Volume 376 (2014)

Cançado Trindade, A. A.: The Contribution of Latin American Legal Doctrine to the Progressive Development of International Law, 9-92.
Gray, C.: The Limits of Force, 93-198.
Najurieta, M. S.: L'adoption internationale des mineurs et les droits de l'enfant, 199-494. (ISBN 978-90-04-29768-5)

Tome/Volume 377 (2015)

Kassir, W. J.: Le renvoi en droit international privé – technique de dialogue entre les cultures juridiques, 9-120.
Noodt Taquela, M. B.: Applying the Most Favourable Treaty or Domestic Rules to Facilitate Private International Law Co-operation, 121-318.
Tuzmukhamedov, B.: Legal Dimensions of Arms Control Agreements, An Introductory Overview, 319-468.
(ISBN 978-90-04-29770-8)

Tome/Volume 378 (2015)

Iwasawa, Y.: Domestic Application of International Law, 9-262.
Carrascosa Gonzalez, J.: The Internet – Privacy and Rights relating to Personality, 263-486. (ISBN 978-90-04-32125-0)

Tome/Volume 379 (2015)

Lowe, V.: The Limits of the Law.
Boele-Woelki, K.: Party Autonomy in Litigation and Arbitration in View of The Hague Principles on Choice of Law in International Commercial Contracts.
Fresnedo de Aguirre, C.: Public Policy: Common Principles in the American States.
Ben Achour, R.: Changements anticonstitutionnels de gouvernement et droit international.
(ISBN 978-90-04-32127-4)

Tome/Volume 380 (2015)

Van Loon, J. H. A.: The Global Horizon of Private International Law.
Pougoué, P.-G.: L'arbitrage dans l'espace OHADA.
Kruger, T.: The Quest for Legal Certainty in International Civil Cases.
(ISBN 978-90-04-32131-1)

Tome/Volume 381 (2015)

Jayme, E.: Les langues et le droit international privé, 11-39.
Bermann, G.: Arbitrage and Private International Law. General Course on Private International Law (2015), 41-484.
(ISBN 978-90-04-33828-9)

Tome/Volume 382 (2015)

Cooper, D., and C. Kuner: Data Protection Law and International Dispute Resolution, 9-174.
Jia, B. B.: International Case Law in the Development of International Law, 175-397.
(ISBN 978-90-04-33830-2)

Tome/Volume 383 (2016)

Bennouna, M.: Le droit international entre la lettre et l'esprit, 9-231.
Iovane, M.: L'influence de la multiplication des juridictions internationales sur l'application du droit international, 233-446.
(ISBN 978-90-04-34648-2)

Tome/Volume 384 (2016)

Symeonides, S. C.: Private International Law Idealism, Pragmatism, Eclecticism, 9-385.
(ISBN 978-90-04-35131-8)

Tome/Volume 385 (2016)

Berman, Sir F.: Why Do we Need a Law of Treaties?, 9-31.
Marrella, F.: Protection internationale des droits de l'homme et activités des sociétés transnationales, 33-435.(ISBN 978-90-04-35132-5)

Tome/Volume 386 (2016)

Murphy, S. D.: International Law relating to Islands, 9-266.
Cataldi, G.: La mise en œuvre des décisions des tribunaux internationaux dans l'ordre interne, 267-428.
(ISBN 978-90-04-35133-2)

Tome/Volume 387 (2016)

Lequette, Y.: Les mutations du droit international privé: vers un changement de paradigme?, 9-644. (ISBN 978-90-04-36118-8)

Tome/Volume 388 (2016)

Bonell, M. J.: The Law Governing International Commercial Contracts: Hard Law versus Soft Law, 9-48.
Hess, B.: The Private-Public Divide in International Dispute Resolution, 49-266.
(ISBN 978-90-04-36120-1)

Tome/Volume 389 (2017)

Muir Watt, H.: Discours sur les méthodes du droit international privé (des formes juridiques de l'inter-altérité). Cours général de droit international privé, 9-410.
(ISBN 978-90-04-36122-5)

Tome/Volume 390 (2017)

Rau, A. S.: The Allocation of Power between Arbitral Tribunals and State Courts, 9-396. (ISBN 978-90-04-36475-2)

Tome/Volume 391 (2017)

Cançado Trindade, A. A. : Les tribunaux internationaux et leur mission commune de réalisation de la justice : développements, état actuel et perspectives, Conférence spéciale (2017), 9-101.
Mariño Menéndez, F. M. : The Prohibition of Torture in Public International Law, 103-185.
Swinarski, C. : Effets pour l'individu des régimes de protection de droit international, 187-369.
Cot, J.-P. : L'éthique du procès international (leçon inaugurale), 371-384.
(ISBN 978-90-04-37781-3)

Tome/Volume 392 (2017)

Novak, F. : The System of Reparations in the Jurisprudence of the Inter-American Court of Human Rights, 9-203.
Nolte, G. : Treaties and their Practice – Symptoms of their Rise or Decline, 205-397. (ISBN 978-90-04-39273-1)

Tome/Volume 393 (2017)

Tiburcio, C. : The Current Practice of International Co-Operation in Civil Matters, 9-310.
Ruiz De Santiago, J. : Aspects juridiques des mouvements forcés de personnes, 311-468.
(ISBN 978-90-04-39274-8)

Tome/Volume 394 (2017)

Kostin, A. A. : International Commercial Arbitration, with Special Focus on Russia, 9-86.
Cuniberti, G. : Le fondement de l'effet des jugements étrangers, 87-283.
(ISBN 978-90-04-39275-5)

Tome/Volume 395 (2018)

Salerno, F. : The Identity and Continuity of Personal Status in Contemporary Private International Law, 9-198.
Chinkin, C. M. : United Nations Accountability for Violations of International Human Rights Law, 199-320. (ISBN 978-90-04-40710-7)

Tome/Volume 396 (2018)

Jacquet, J.-M. : Droit international privé et arbitrage commercial international, 9-36.
Brown Weiss, E. : Establishing Norms in a Kaleidoscopic World. General Course on Public International Law, 37-415. (ISBN 978-90-04-41002-2)

Tome/Volume 397 (2018)

D'Avout, L. : L'entreprise et les conflits internationaux de lois, 9-612.
(ISBN 978-90-04-41221-7)

Tome/Volume 398 (2018)

Treves, T. : The Expansion of International Law, General Course on Public International Law (2015), 9-398. (ISBN 978-90-04-41224-8)

Tome/Volume 399 (2018)

Kanehara, A.: Reassessment of the Acts of the State in the Law of State Responsibility, 9-266.
Buxbaum, H. L.: Public Regulation and Private Enforcement in a Global Economy: Strategies for Managing Conflict, 267-442. (ISBN 978-90-04-41670-3)

Tome/Volume 400 (2018)

Chedly, L.: L'efficacité de l'arbitrage commercial international, 9-624. (ISBN 978-90-04-42388-6)

Tome/Volume 401 (2019)

Wood, P.: Extraterritorial Enforcement of Regulatory Laws, 9-126.
Nishitani, Yuko: Identité culturelle en droit international privé de la famille, 127-450. (ISBN 978-90-04-42389-3)

Tome/Volume 402 (2019)

Kinsch, P.: Le rôle du politique en droit international privé. Cours général de droit international privé, 9-384.
Dasser, F.: "Soft Law" in International Commercial Arbitration, 385-596. (ISBN 978-90-04-42392-3)

Tome/Volume 403 (2019)

Daudet, Y.: 1919-2019, le flux du multilatéralisme, 9-48.
Kessedjian, C.: Le tiers impartial et indépendant en droit international, juge, arbitre, médiateur, conciliateur, 49-643. (ISBN 978-90-04-42468-5)

Tome/Volume 404 (2019)

Rajamani, L.: Innovation and Experimentation in the International Climate Change Regime, 9-234.
Sorel, J.-M.: Quelle normativité pour le droit des relations monétaires et financières internationales?, 235-403. (ISBN 978-90-04-43142-3)

Tome/Volume 405 (2019)

Paulsson, J.: Issues arising from Findings of Denial of Justice, 9-74.
Brunée, J.: Procedure and Substance in International Environmental Law, 75-240. (ISBN 978-90-04-43300-7)

Tome/Volume 406 (2019)

Bundy, R.: The Practice of International Law, Inaugural Lecture, 9-26.
Gama, L.: Les principes d'UNIDROIT et la loi régissant les contrats de commerce, 27-343. (ISBN 978-90-04-43611-4)

Tome/Volume 407 (2020)

Wouters, J.: Le statut juridique des standards publics et privés dans les relations économiques internationales, 9-122.
Maljean-Dubois, S.: Le droit international de la biodiversité, 123-538. (ISBN 978-90-04-43643-5)

Tome/Volume 408 (2020)

Cançado Trindade, A. A.: Reflections on the Realization of Justice in the Era of Contemporary International Tribunals, 9-88.
González, C.: Party Autonomy in International Family Law, 89-361.
(ISBN 978-90-04-44504-8)

Tome/Volume 409 (2020)

Shany, Y: The Extraterritorial Application of International Human Rights Law, 9-152.
Besson, S.: La *due diligence* en droit international, 153-398.
(ISBN 978-90-04-44505-5)

Tome/Volume 410 (2020)

Koh, H. H.: American Schools of International Law, 9-93.
Peters, A.: Animals in International Law, 95-544. (ISBN 978-90-04-44897-1)

Tome/Volume 411 (2020)

Cahin, G: Reconstrution et construction de l'Etat en droit international, 9-573.
(ISBN 978-90-04-44898-8)

Tome/Volume 412 (2020)

Momtaz, D: La hiérarchisation de l'ordre juridique international, cours général de droit international public, 9-252.
Grammaticaki-Alexiou, A.: Best Interests of the Child in Private International Law, 253-434.
(ISBN 978-90-04-44899-5)

Tome/Volume 413 (2021)

Ferrari, F.: Forum Shopping Despite Unification of Law, 9-290.
(ISBN 978-90-04-46100-0)

Tome/Volume 414 (2021)

Pellet, A.: Le droit international à la lumière de la pratique: l'introuvable théorie de la réalité. Cours général de droit international public, 9-547.
(ISBN 978-90-04-46547-3)

Tome/Volume 415 (2021)

Trooboff, P. D.: Globalization, Personal Jurisdiction and the Internet. Responding to the Challenge of adapting settled Principles and Precedents. General Course of Private International Law, 9-321.
(ISBN 978-90-04-46730-9)

Tome/Volume 416 (2021)

Wolfrum, R: Solidarity and Community Interests: Driving Forces for the Interpretation and Development of International Law. General Course on Public International Law, 9-479. (ISBN 978-90-04-46827-6)

Tome/Volume 417 (2021)

d'Argent, P.: Les obligations internationales, 9-210.
Schabas, W. A.: Relationships Between International Criminal Law and Other Branches of International Law, 211-392. (ISBN 978-90-04-47239-6)

Tome/Volume 418 (2021)

Bollée, S.: Les pouvoirs inhérents des arbitres internationaux, 9-224.
Tladi, D.: The Extraterritorial Use of Force against Non-State Actors, 225-360. (ISBN 978-90-04-50380-9)

Tome/Volume 419 (2021)

Kolb, R.: Le droit international comme corps de «droit privé» et de «droit public». Cours général de droit international public, 9-668. (ISBN 978-90-04-50381-6)

Tome/Volume 420 (2021)

Perrakis, S.: La protection internationale au profit des personnes vulnérables en droit international des droits de l'homme, 9-497. (ISBN 978-90-04-50382-3)

Tome/Volume 421 (2021)

Estrella Faria, J. A.: La protection des biens culturels d'intérêt religieux en droit international public et en droit international privé, 9-333. (ISBN 978-90-04-50829-3)

Tome/Volume 422 (2021)

Karayanni, M.: The Private International Law of Class Actions: A Functional approach, 9-248.
Mahmoudi, S.: Self-Defence and "Unwilling or Unable" States, 249-399. (ISBN 978-90-04-50830-9)

Tome/Volume 423 (2022)

Kinnear, M.: The Growth, Challenges and Future Prospects for Investment Dispute Settlement, 9-36.
Weller, M.: "Mutual Trust": A Suitable Foundation for Private International Law in Regional Integration Communities and Beyond?, 37-378. (ISBN 978-90-04-51411-9)

Tome/Volume 424 (2022)

Asada, M.: International Law of Nuclear Non-proliferation and Disarmament, 9-726. (ISBN 978-90-04-51769-1)

Tome/Volume 425 (2022)

Metou, B. M.: Le contrôle international des dérogations aux droits de l'homme, 9-294.
Silva Romero, E.: Legal Fictions in the Language of International Arbitration, 295-423. (ISBN 978-90-04-51770-7)

Tome/Volume 426 (2022)

Kuijper, P. J.: Delegation and International Organizations, 9-240.
McCaffrey, S. C.: The Evolution of the Law of International Watercourses, 241-384.

(ISBN 978-90-04-51771-4)

Tome/Volume 427 (2022)

Kaufmann-Kohler, G.: Indépendance et impartialité du juge et de l'arbitre dans le règlement des différends entre investisseurs et Etats (leçon inaugurale), 9-50.
Boyle, A.: International Lawmaking in an Environmental Context, 51-108.
Weller, M.-P.: La méthode tripartite du droit international privé: désignation, reconnaissance, considération, 109-210.
Mourre, A.: La légitimité de l'arbitrage, 211-288.

(ISBN 978-90-04-52770-6)

Tome/Volume 428 (2023)

Laghmani, S.: Islam et droit international, 9-128.
Oyarzábal, M. J. A.: The Influence of Public International Law upon Private International Law in History and Theory and in the Formation and Application of the Law, 129-525.

(ISBN 978-90-04-54440-6)

Tome/Volume 429 (2023)

Moreno Rodríguez, J. A.: Private (And Public) International Law In Investment Arbitration, 9-702.

(ISBN 978-90-04-54462-8)

Tome/Volume 430 (2023)

Casella, P. B.: Droit international, histoire et culture, 9-610.

(ISBN 978-90-04-54463-5)

Tome/Volume 431 (2023)

Yeo, T. M.: Common Law, Equity and Statute. The Effect of Juridical Sources on Choice-of-Law Methodology, 9-88.
Frigessi Di Rattalma, M.: New Trends in Private International Law of Insurance Contracts, 89-200
Roosevelt III, K.: The Third Restatement of Conflict of Laws, 201-284
Sands, P.: Colonialism: A Short History of International Law in Five Acts, 285-410

(ISBN 978-90-04-54464-2)

LES LIVRES DE POCHE DE L'ACADÉMIE

(Par ordre chronologique de parution)

1

Gaillard, E.: Aspects philosophiques du droit de l'arbitrage international, 2008, 252 pages. (ISBN 978-90-04-17148-0)

2

Schrijver, N.: The Evolution of Sustainable Development in International Law: Inception, Meaning and Status, 2008, 276 pages. (ISBN 978-90-04-17407-8)

3

Moura Vicente, D.: La propriété intellectuelle en droit international privé, 2009, 516 pages.

(ISBN 978-90-04-17907-3)

4

Decaux, E.: Les formes contemporaines de l'esclavage, 2009, 272 pages. (ISBN 978-90-04-17908-0)

5

McLachlan, C.: Lis Pendens in International Litigation, 2009, 492 pages. (ISBN 978-90-04-17909-7)

6

Carbone, S. M.: Conflits de lois en droit maritime, 2010, 312 pages. (ISBN 978-90-04-18688-0)

7

Boele-Woelki, K.: Unifying and Harmonizing Substantive Law and the Role of Conflict of Laws, 2010, 288 pages.

(ISBN 978-90-04-18683-5)

8

Onuma, Y.: A Transcivilizational Perspective in International Law, 2010, 492 pages. (ISBN 978-90-04-18689-7)

9

Bucher, A.: La dimension sociale du droit international privé. Cours général, 2011, 552 pages. (ISBN 978-90-04-20917-6)

10

Thürer, D.: International Humanitarian Law: Theory, Practice, Context, 2011, 504 pages. (ISBN 978-90-04-17910-3)

11

Alvarez, J. E.: The Public International Law Regime Governing International Investment, 2011, 504 pages.

(ISBN 978-90-04-18682-8)

12

Wang, G.: Radiating Impact of WTO on Its Members' Legal System: The Chinese Perspective, 2011, 384 pages.

(ISBN 978-90-04-21854-3)

13

Bogdan, M.: Private International Law as Component of the Law of the Forum, 2012, 360 pages. (ISBN 978-90-04-22634-0)

14

Davey, W. J.: Non-discrimination in the World Trade Organization: The Rules and Exceptions, 2012, 360 pages. (ISBN 978-90-04-23314-0)

15

Xue Hanqin: Chinese Contemporary Perspectives on International Law — History, Culture and International Law, 2012, 288 pages.
(ISBN 978-90-04-23613-4)

16

Reisman, W. M.: The Quest for World Order and Human Dignity in the Twenty-first Century: Constitutive Process and Individual Commitment. General Course on Public International Law, 2012, 504 pages.
(ISBN 978-90-04-23615-8)

17

Dugard, J.: The Secession of States and Their Recognition in the Wake of Kosovo, 2013, 312 pages.
(ISBN 978-90-04-25748-1)

18

Gannagé, L.: Les méthodes du droit international privé à l'épreuve des conflits de cultures, 2013, 372 pages.
(ISBN 978-90-04-25750-4)

19

Kohler, Ch.: L'autonomie de la volonté en droit international privé : un principe universel entre libéralisme et étatisme, 2013, 288 pages.
(ISBN 978-90-04-25752-8)

20

Kreindler, R.: Competence-Competence in the Face of Illegality in Contracts and Arbitration Agreements, 2013, 504 pages.
(ISBN 978-90-04-25754-2)

21

Crawford, J.: Chance, Order, Change: The Course of International Law. General Course on Public International Law, 2014, 540 pages.
(ISBN 978-90-04-26808-1)

22

Brand, R. A.: Transaction Planning Using Rules on Jurisdiction and the Recognition and Enforcement of Judgments, 2014, 360 pages.
(ISBN 978-90-04-26810-4)

23

Kolb, R.: L'article 103 de la Charte des Nations Unies, 2014, 416 pages.
(ISBN 978-90-04-27836-3)

24

Benvenisti, E.: The Law of Global Governance, 2014, 336 pages.
(ISBN 978-90-04-27911-7)

25

Yusuf, A. A.: Pan-Africanism and International Law, 2014, 288 pages.
(ISBN 978-90-04-28504-0)

26

Kono, T.: Efficiency in Private International Law, 2014, 216 pages.
(ISBN 978-90-04-28506-4)

27

Cachard, O., Le transport international aérien de passagers, 2015, 292 pages. (ISBN 978-90-04-29773-9)

28

Corten, O.: La rébellion et le droit international, 2015, 376 pages. (ISBN 978-90-04-29775-3)

29

Frigo, M., Circulation des biens culturels, détermination de la loi applicable et méthodes de règlement des litiges, 2016, 552 pages. (ISBN 978-90-04-32129-8)

30

Bermann, G. A., International Arbitration and Private International Law, 2017, 648 pages. (ISBN 978-90-04-34825-7)

31

Bennouna, M., Le droit international entre la lettre et l'esprit, 2017, 304 pages. (ISBN 978-90-04-34846-2)

32

Murphy, S., International Law relating to Islands, 376 pages. (ISBN 978-90-04-36154-6)

33

Hess, B., The Private-Public Law Divide in International Dispute Resolution, 328 pages. (ISBN 978-90-04-38490-3)

34

Rau, A.: The Allocation of Power between Arbitral Tribunals and State Courts, 2018, 608 pages. (ISBN 978-90-04-38891-8)

35

Muir Watt, H.: Discours sur les méthodes du droit international privé (des formes juridiques de l'inter-altérité, 2019, 608 pages. (ISBN 978-90-04-39558-9)

36

Nolte, G.: Treaties and Their Practice – Symptoms of Their Rise or Decline, 2018, 288 pages. (ISBN 978-90-04-39456-8)

37

Cuniberti, G.: Le fondement de l'effet des jugements étrangers, 2019, 288 pages. (ISBN 978-90-04-41180-7)

38

D'Avout, L.: L'entreprise et les conflits internationaux de lois, 875 pages. (ISBN 978-90-04-41668-0)

39

Brown Weiss, E.: Establishing Norms in a Kaleidoscopic World, 528 pages. (ISBN 978-90-04-42200-1)

40

Brunnée, J.: Procedure and Substance in International Environmental Law, 2020, 240 pages. (ISBN 978-90-04-44437-9)

41
Rajamani, L.: Innovation and Experimentation in the International Climate Change Regime, 2020, 336 pages.
(ISBN 978-90-04-44439-3)

42
Kessedjian, C.: Le tiers impartial et indépendant en droit international, juge, arbitre, médiateur, conciliateur, 2020, 832 pages. (ISBN 978-90-04-44880-3)

43
Maljean-Dubois, S.: Le droit international de la biodiversité, 2021, 590 pages.
(ISBN 978-90-04-46287-8)

44
Dasser, F.: "Soft Law" in International Commercial Arbitration, 2021, 300 pages.
(ISBN 978-90-04-46289-2)

45
Peters, A.: Animals in International Law, 2021, 641 pages.
(ISBN 978-90-04-46624-1)

46
Besson, S.: La *due diligence* en droit international, 2021, 363 pages.
(ISBN 978-90-04-46626-5)

47
Ferrari, F.: Forum Shopping Despite Unification of Law, 2021, 446 pages.
(ISBN 978-90-04-46626-5)

48
Wolfrum, R.: Solidarity and Community Interests: Driving Forces for the Interpretation and Development of International Law, 2021, 663 pages.
(ISBN 978-90-04-50832-3)

49
Kolb, R.: Le droit international comme corps de « droit privé » et de « droit public », 2022, 976 pages.
(ISBN 978-90-04-51836-0)

50
Tladi, D.: The Extraterritorial Use of Force against Non-State Actors, 2022, 208 pages.
(ISBN 978-90-04-52147-6)

51
Schabas, W. A.: Relationships between International Criminal Law and Other Branches of International Law, 2022, 272 pages.
(ISBN 978-90-04-52149-0)

52
Bollée, S.: Les pouvoirs inhérents des arbitres internationaux, 2023, 306 pages.
(ISBN 978-90-04-67848-4)

53
Laghmani, S.: Islam et droit international, 2023, 168 pages.
(ISBN 978-90-04-67850-7)